The Fire Within

Shedding Light on Trauma

You can find us at https://firewithin.online

or

on Facebook as TheFireWithin22.

Cover Credits:
    Photographer ~ Ben Altenes ~ BenAltenesPhoto.com
    The Face on the Cover ~ Joshua Allred
    Cover Editors ~ Alex Vance ~ Mat Vance

Original Idea of the Book
    Grant Rogers

Book Narrator and Organizer:
    Mat Vance

Authors:

Amy Miner	Joshua Luke
Brandon Tennery	K. Brown
Crazy Horse 6	Kevin "Mac" McEnneny
D. Alex Wilson	Mat Vance
Dana Brown	Michael Mather
David Rogers	Nathan "Thumper" Johnson
Grant Rogers	Nelson Smith
Jake Jourdonnais	Phillip M. Chavez
John Francisco	Phillip Trezza
Joseph R. Faulkner	Pitch
Joshua D. LeBel	Shep

In honor of those we've lost, this is for the ones we can still reach.

You are not alone.

DEFINING THE FIRE WITHIN US

Flames are alive, for they dance and glow even as they consume. They are a mesmerizing beauty which has attracted the attention of man since the beginning of time. It is pointless to consider a world without fire, for there would be no world to consider. All of life and society revolves around the flames; for their warmth, their energy, their purity and their grace. And as we have grown, as a society, we have used these traits to better our existence. Our houses are heated by combusting coal and our cars by burning oil. We look up at the sun's inferno and the very cells of our body respond. But what is it that allows for this? What do the embers in the fireplace have in common with a star? It is combustion, the release of energy that others may use. Some would say that this is destructive, that fire burns from a fuel that is used and must eventually run out. This is true. But of greater truth is that for the burning of the flame we are able to construct much more; that the flames allow us to see in the dark and guide our path, keep us warm when we are cold, give us that energy which we turn into strength and allow us to accomplish that which would be impossible without. The flames are alive because fire is life.

~ John Oxendine ~

TABLE OF CONTENTS

FOREWORD

Bill Rausch

Everyone has a story.

It's one of the things that makes us human, and humans have shared stories since the beginning of time. Regardless of where we come from, who we are, or what we do for a living, if we could all share our stories, we would likely find more in common with each other than we would expect.

For me, my story includes service to my country in the U.S. military. Because of this service, I am by definition, a veteran.

There are 21.8 million other Americans whose service also warrants the label of veteran. Like any label, "veteran" often conjures a certain image in a person's mind. That image is usually based on what they've seen in the movies, television, or media. What many do not realize is that being a veteran isn't my, or any veteran's, entire story.

In addition to being a veteran, I am the first in my family to graduate from a four-year college; I am a proud father and husband; I volunteer in my local community in Alexandria, Virginia; and I lead a national nonprofit organization focused on veteran empowerment, called Got Your 6. Despite serving in uniform for more than a decade, including my time as a cadet at West Point, I've actually spent the majority of my life outside the military. Being a veteran is an important chapter of my life, but it's certainly not the whole book.

Unfortunately, most Americans have preconceived perceptions of veterans that tend to fall on extreme ends of the spectrum. Some are positive, aka "hero," and some are negative, typically "damaged." The fact is, veterans are as diverse as the country we serve. Racially and ethnically, for the most part, the veteran population closely reflects the American population and while the veteran population remains heavily male, women are the fastest growing population of veterans and now total almost 11 percent of all veterans, including 20 percent of veterans under the age of 50.

It has been my general sense and experience that as a nation, we are overwhelmingly supportive of our military and our men and women who transition back to small towns and big cities across the country. I experienced it first hand when I came home from Iraq after being gone for nearly 17 months.

I remember touching down at the airport in Dallas and getting off the plane. I was in uniform, carrying my flight bag, excited to get back to Fort Sill, Oklahoma, where my family and friends were waiting to welcome us home. As I exited the aircraft with my fellow passengers, around a hundred people were there to welcome us home. People I didn't know and had never met were cheering as we walked off the plane. They shook my hand, they embraced me and they thanked me for my service. I was emotional, not realizing people could be so grateful. At the same time, I felt guilty for receiving such praise and appreciation while thinking of my brothers and sisters in arms who had given so much more of themselves to the fight; many losing limbs and some even losing their lives. Those men and women sacrificed so much more than me, and I didn't feel that I deserved anyone's praise or thanks. I know now this is a common feeling.

It wasn't until I connected with fellow veterans in my community at a weekly run with Team Red, White and Blue (RWB) that I finally started to feel a part of something bigger than myself. I found that lost sense of camaraderie. The experience was so powerful that I started a Team RWB Chapter in my local community of Alexandria, VA. I quickly found myself volunteering more than 20 hours a week, organizing events and reaching out to veteran and civilian members in my community. Over long runs, learning to rock climb and sharing stories, I realized I wasn't the only one longing to go back to a combat zone. I also realized I had more in common with other veterans and civilians than I realized by getting to know them better, listening to their stories and asking them questions. I also learned nearly all of us had experienced trauma in life, in and out of uniform, and we could help each other through the tough times. We could empower each other to bring about the good times. For the first time in years I found myself building genuine and trusted relationships with my fellow citizens and that is what put me on the path to a successful transition not only out of the military, but in my life.

Volunteering with Team RWB changed my life. It connected me to my community and allowed me to place a higher priority on wellness and ultimately inspired me to leave my career in government contracting. It eventually led me to *Got Your 6*, where I serve as Executive Director. I am fortunate enough to not only work with veterans, but more importantly, to empower veterans to lead in their communities. It's a fact that civic engagement is on the decline across the nation. However, given that veterans vote, volunteer and are generally more active in their communities, the mission of Got Your 6 serves the veteran as well as the entire nation; to empower veterans to lead a resurgence of community across the nation!

Through our work, I get to travel across the country meeting people from all walks of life and hear their stories. Sometimes I share parts of my own story, hopeful I will inspire others and also remind myself how much I have in common with my fellow Americans. I've cried with strangers when talking about living with post-traumatic stress and embraced those who have lost friends and family to suicide.

The storytellers you are about to read about are as diverse as the country we served and being a veteran is just part of our story. We are many things. Fathers. Sons. Mothers. Daughters. Volunteers. Entrepreneurs. Community Leaders. Civic Assets. And yes, we also happen to be veterans. It may have been difficult for the authors of the stories in this book to put pen to paper, and I hope you, the reader, appreciate their bravery, humor and insights. I hope this collection urges you to share your story and recognize that as Americans, we often have more in common than we may think.

As we say in the Army: One team, one fight.

PREFACE

Though war has been raging since the dawn of humankind, the study of trauma experienced in battle is still leaving us with questions. What do we call the symptoms that come from trauma? Some will say Post Traumatic Stress (PTS) and others will say Post Traumatic Stress Disorder (PTSD). One big thing often overlooked, especially since 2001 when we sent troops to Afghanistan and then in 2003 to Iraq, is the fact that PTS(D) is not just for veterans and not all veterans experience trauma while overseas.

PTS(D) is for all humans that experience traumatic events, such as car crash victims or sexual assault victims just to mention the tip of the iceberg. By placing the word "veteran" next to "PTSD" since 2001, the veteran and civilian communities ostracize each other. One group has scary stories that the other group doesn't understand, yet both groups need each other because at the end of the day, we're all humans that can be effected by trauma. Veterans volunteered to get their hands dirty while civilians enjoyed their freedoms. On the other hand, veterans need the support of the civilian community before, during and after each deployment. We need each other. So how can we work together to shed light on the subject matter? We simply speak to each other to understand what's really going on within us. When problems are identified, we can work together to solve them a lot quicker than we have been.

This book is a collection of opinions alongside some research. There are combatants that have served in the U.S. Army, Marines, Navy, Air Force and the independent security contracting world in the pages ahead. Some know each other like family. Others have no clue who any of the other writers are. Some were on the same deployment and others were deployed to completely different places in completely different years. We even have the point of view from a wife of a veteran and how she handled their struggle. Each writer was asked, as a guideline, to write about their opinions of PTS(D) before seeing combat and their opinions on the subject matter after combat. Every single writer interpreted the task differently... even if they stood by another one of the writers in combat, experiencing the exact same events. Their individual opinions will show how there's a lot more to the diagnosis of PTS(D) than we have previously thought.

KINDLING & THE SPARK

How did this project come about? My name is Mat Vance and I had the honor of serving with a lot of great people while in the military and security contracting world, to include Grant Rogers. He approached me about an idea in 2014. Grant really wanted to work on a book that would help veterans with PTS(D). I told him that sounded like a good idea and I was actually working on another book as well. About a year later in 2015, I released my book, "The Funny Side of War." After inquiring about how my book developed from an idea to a finished piece, Grant asked if I wanted to get involved with his book. I obliged and we agreed that we wanted to gather veterans that had seen combat. We also wanted veterans from different branches as well as veterans that had served in the same platoon. This would offer the reader a wide spectrum of viewpoints while veterans gave their opinions on the subject of PTS(D) based on their individual experiences. We would then take a look at what everyone had written to see how we could piece together a book that would benefit veterans, civilians that are curious about what veterans have experienced and all people that have experienced different levels of trauma in their lives.

Throughout 2016, Grant and I received possible book entries from dozens of veterans. We vetted each person to make sure what they had written was valid. After 3 years of forming ideas and finding the right people, we found enough kindling to start the fire! Once we finalized this diverse group of authors, we debated on how much to edit their entries during the editing process. I made decisions on a page-by-page basis to ensure the integrity of the writer's voice was maintained. I felt it was necessary to leave some writing blemishes to accomplish this. As you read their stories, you will notice slight differences in each author as they transition from their opinion of PTS(D) before combat, after combat and reflecting on their time served overall as it relates to their current lives.

Who's involved in this project? The authors have served in different branches of the military. There are officers and enlisted members. There are authors who were infantry, medics, scouts, intelligence, support, forward observers, artillery, mortars, a SEAL, security contractors and a veteran's wife. An author was shot in the face. An author lost a leg. An author lost a best friend. An author sustained a traumatic brain injury. An author lost a husband. All of the authors have seen tragedies of war.

Some of the authors wrote about PTS(D) in a cynical fashion, while others wrote in a positive manner. Their styles of writing range from scattered thoughts to college style papers to describing dreams to poetry. For some, this is the first time they have spoken about their opinions and experiences. They provided the spark that lit this fire within.

Authors in this project will be donating a percentage of their proceeds to the following organizations:

Fisher House (Shep and Joshua D. LeBel)
Got Your 6 (Crazy Horse 6)
The Invictus Games (D. Alex Wilson)
Operation Comfort (D. Alex Wilson)
Wishes for Warriors (Jake Jourdonnais)
TAPS: Tragedy Assistance Program for Survivors (K. Brown)
Heroes Sports (Grant Rogers)
The Gary Sinise Foundation (Amy Miner)
The Josh Pallotta Fund (Amy Miner)
Southeastern Guide Dogs (Nelson Smith)
Virginia Veteran's Services Foundation (Phillip Trezza)
Minnesota Warriors Disabled Veteran's Hockey Program (Dana Brown)

Chalk Talk

"Chalk" is military jargon for a small group of troops that are loaded up and ready to jump out of a perfectly fine helicopter or plane en route to the unknown. They are mentally and physically prepared to do what is necessary to complete the mission, but they also know plans typically go to shit as soon as they hit the ground. That defines each of these writers. They know they have stories and experiences that will help people, but they are still taking a big leap by opening up in such a public way.

There are 3 chalks in this book with unique individual stories in-between. Each chalk will have its own aspect that is different from the others. This will give you a look at many points of view on the subject of PTS(D) by people that have experienced traumatic events.

CHALK ONE

The first group contains the stories of 6 members of the United States Army. They don't know each other. They served in different places at different times. They will take you from an invasion, to being shot in the face, to losing a leg in an IED (improvised explosive device) attack, to unimaginable internal injuries, to philosophical views, to cynical and positive outlooks and to pushing forward. Their words are raw with brutal honesty.

IN FRONT OF THE LINE

Joseph R. Faulkner

This piece is a reflection on my struggles with Post Traumatic Stress Disorder (PTSD). I was hospitalized and diagnosed with PTSD in June of 2014. I don't entirely believe that society understands those with PTSD and some people are quick to classify the disorder as a crazy, mental illness, which is not the case. We are no different from anyone else. We have just witnessed or had to do things that aren't normal in American culture. The struggle with PTSD in veterans is very real, and I did not think that I would have made it this far in treatment if it weren't for others just like me. This is the very first time that I have shared any information outside of my veteran circle. I hope that you enjoy what you read.

*　　*　　*

As I sat in an unfamiliar place listening to others share experiences and revisiting the darkest places inside my mind, I realized that I was not alone and I was not willing to suffer any longer. I had to make it to the other side.

In 2002, I was assigned to a brigade reconnaissance troop in the 3rd Infantry Division (3ID). We were deployed to Kuwait in August on a normal rotation that eventually turned into preparing equipment and waiting for orders to invade Iraq. On March 17, 2003, we received an operation brief on our actual role during the invasion, which was textbook reconnaissance passing through DIV CAV (Division Cavalry) after the 2nd day. During the brief, the commander made it clear that the objective was Baghdad, a city with a population of over 8 million people. I was barely in my early twenties, but in my mind, I was ready.

The Division was nice enough to give us a surgeon. Our unit was approximately 16 trucks and 40 personnel, plus attachments. On March 20, 2003, we went across the Iraqi border and set a screen line for DIV CAV. The next morning, we conducted a passage of lines with them and took the lead. I

3

remember thinking that we are the most northern American forces in Iraq and there will be no chance of me mistaking the enemy for friendly units. I was steady on my machine gun for several days through various forms of contact (interactions with the enemy). Depending on the size of the enemy, we would either push through them or wait on the Task Force following closely behind to sweep the objective, then regain the lead. We had a front seat through the carnage of war. There are no words to express the sight of an innocent family of four destroyed by a .50 cal machine gun.

By the time we approached the Euphrates River I was drenched in sweat from wearing a chemical suit in the desert heat. My hands were so dry and rough from the sand in the air that they were starting to crack. We confirmed that there were Iraqi tanks dug in just across the river as we waited for the Task Force (TF). The TF approached, things exploded and they swept the objective, destroying everything that moved. We picked up and continued north through the objective to find a route into Baghdad. One of the following mornings we were approaching an intersection where there were abandoned civilian and enemy vehicles, some still running. We made a left turn and all hell broke loose. We were ambushed from a few different directions. Civilians ran for cover, bullets flew and sweat dripped into my eyes all while returning fire into trees that were less than 15 feet in front of us. A minute seemed like an hour. After it was all over I thought, "Man, that was a close call." We continued to have head-on collisions with death for the next few weeks, all the way into the heart of Baghdad. After the "Thunder Runs" (American armored attacks) and once Baghdad fell, we had a few weeks to breathe. I had time to think.

I was lucky enough to make it that far and to be still alive, so I started to replay all of my engagements again inside my mind and question the decisions I had made. Seeing what a human can do to another person, I questioned myself and I questioned God. I have been to several scary haunted houses, but none of them compare to what we witness in war. Those images never leave you... you never forget. All you can do is try to move on and at that time we did. At that age, it doesn't really get to you.

After a brief time in Baghdad, we fought on into Fallujah. Fighting in Fallujah was like fighting a completely different war. The enemy's tactics were well organized and they attacked with precision. Around this time, we started to see the use of IEDs (Improvised Explosive Devices) and VBIEDs (Vehicle Born IED or "car bomb"). We continued the fight in the Fallujah area until it was time to go home.

There is something that changes in the mind of a soldier when he survives death over and over again. I may have destroyed the enemy, but I also may have destroyed innocent families. At a young age, I was given permission to play God and decide whether people lived or died. Once I returned to the United States, I began to have problems. They started with intrusive thoughts, memories and nightmares. I pushed my wife and family away. I waged an internal war in my soul trying to justify my actions, what I shot at, if I was sure I didn't accidentally hit friendlies or for God sakes, a child. For this reason, I turned to the only thing that I knew would melt the anxiety; alcohol. For many years, it was my answer to deal with the internal battle. I used it as a tool to forget.

I became numb inside, experiencing the things that I did and having to bury them immediately, only to continue the mission. I kept my wife locked out from knowing what I was particularly going through; I pushed her away. I slowly became dead inside and lost all empathy for others. I was no longer comfortable in a peaceful environment, so I continued to chase deployments. I ended up going to Korea.

After Korea, I chased another tour back to Iraq in 2007-2008. We could no longer move freely and had an enormous number of rules that we had to follow. I slowly became aware that this would be slightly more dangerous than my previous deployment due to the fact we were sitting ducks in the middle of the Ahdamiya/Sadr City area. This tour was so intense for me because of the AO (Area of Operation) and its length of 14 straight months. One of our units in Baghdad was losing good men at a rate that no group had experienced since the Vietnam War. Our Squadron shifted over and replaced that unit. Coming into that area, for the first few months, I started to wonder if I would ever make it home. I eventually made it out

5

and back home. This time my soul was completely dead.

I was an excellent combat soldier. I passed the selection process to be an Army Green Beret. I went into Special Forces training after that '07 - '08 tour in Iraq. I excelled in that environment, because the switch inside my brain was stuck on full throttle. I had become so stuck in that mindset that it cost me my marriage and I left a son without his father for a couple of years.

Through the years, always putting the mission first, I thought it was just part of being a combat hardened soldier. It was normal to apply combat instincts to civilian life, such as watching my environment or needing to control every little thing around me. I would avoid large crowds and had problems in social situations where the smallest of things would set me off. I felt like I had unquestionably no connection to another person outside of the military.

I transferred to Fort Polk, Louisiana, at the end of 2013 and that is when it all came crashing down. I was no longer able to be in the environment that made me feel safe. The Army slowed down, but I did not. I started having trouble with short-term memory. I would sit on my couch with a 1,000-yard stare on my face. Somebody could be sitting next to me, and I would not hear a word they said. My life became unmanageable because there was too much silence and downtime. It enabled my mind to use the world as a canvas to paint the horrible pictures that have stayed in my mind. I struggled to stay out of trouble both with the Army and local law enforcement, mostly due to my alcohol abuse.

I entered treatment in June of 2014 and it has been a long uphill fight since then. One thing I noticed about myself in battling PTSD is that I do not have to keep fighting it. I always needed to let it go and not let it run my life. The only thing I needed to do was manage the behaviors and notice them before they get out of hand.

Living with a person with PTSD is extremely difficult. Relationships become volatile and everyone walks on eggshells around us. We live in constant conflict trying to manage PTSD. Sometimes we may say things or do things that are emotionally hurtful to others, but in our hearts, we do not mean them. The

6

best way to emotionally connect with us is to give us our space and when we are ready, we will come to you.

Through treatment, I have learned how to let go, manage depression and anxiety, as well as reconnect with a typical person. Therapy and medicine only get us so far. Our recovery depends solely on us and our willingness to seek help. Anyone suffering from PTSD should seek help. The longer you wait, the worse it gets and the more suffering you cause others. At the end of our service, we become a number and get released into society. Is it worth that much that we are willing to suck it up and not get help? Are we ready to self-destruct to the point where we lose everything, even our life, just to avoid a label? I chose to put my career on the line just to save my life. Treatment will never stop for me because I will always remember everything. However, it is how we interpret those memories that determine if we can manage life.

THE TASTE OF COPPER

Michael Mather

My name is SGT (sergeant) Michael Mather. I am the youngest of three boys. I was born in Ohio where I began working at the age of 6 with paper routes before school and cutting grass or raking leaves. My father, as many of my family before him, served in the military. My family has a long history of serving this country from the beginning. We fought in the Revolutionary War and every war since. I have had all the ideals instilled in me since I can remember. I have always wanted to serve my nation and two weeks after I graduated high school, I left for boot camp. I started off in the U.S. Air Force as an F-15 mechanic and rose through the ranks to E-5. When I hit my 9th year in the Air Force I decided to move over to the Army where I thought I might feel more useful. I wanted to actually contribute to the war and new freedoms of the people in less fortunate countries.

On July 27, 2007, I became SGT Mather of the U.S. Army. I enlisted as an FO or F.I.S.T or Fire Support Specialist, which basically meant myself, along with 6 other men in a squad, would be the eyes of the Artillery. My first unit with the Army was the greatest in my mind. I was now a part of the 10th Mountain, 4th Brigade, 3rd Squadron, 86 Cavalry, stationed out of Ft. Polk, Louisiana. Otherwise known as hell to many soldiers for this is the place where a lot of units went through JRTC (Joint Readiness Training Center), a place where they had to train for a month before deploying. I arrived at Polk at the end of October, 2007. When I got there, I was informed my unit was slotted for deployment. When I finally got my wife to Polk from my previous duty station, I had to break the news to her that I would be boots-on-ground in 19 days.

I had just enough time to get her there and the house set up before leaving her there without knowing anyone. She was all alone while I had the daunting task of deploying with a bunch of guys who had no idea who I was or what I was capable of doing for them. So, the first few months were very difficult because I was an NCO (non-commissioned officer) with the knowledge of an E-fuzzy (low ranking Army member). I was tasked with radio watch in the TOC (tactical operations center) at night, which did not bother me because it gave me the chance to learn all the SOP's (standard operating procedures) and the men and women that were there. Once I got the idea and felt comfortable, I asked if I could start going on patrols. At first I was denied, told I was "needed" in the TOC and I was being tossed around from the FOB (forward operating base) to the JSS (joint surveillance system) to doing other little tasks they needed. But then I asked if I could go out on my own time and they agreed.

At night, I was the radio guy and after my shift was over and in between my other duties and tasks I was given, I would go out on as many patrols as I could. I was only getting maybe 3 hours of sleep a day, because I was addicted to the adrenalin of being outside the gate. I did this for about 5 months or so before they put me into a platoon for good and then I was going out on patrols all the time and only filling in for others on the radio when they absolutely needed it, which was not often.

My first encounter with "war" was actually doing my job as an FO. I was in the TOC while my guys were out pulling security for the engineers who were putting up the barriers along routes south and north of Baghdad, an area known as "The Five Fingers of Death." I was using the camera on the blimps we had in country at that time. I came across one man digging a hole and placing an IED just a short way ahead of where my guys were. My platoon sergeant, SFC Milstead, and I were watching as I got the 10-digit grid and called it up to my FSO, who then called it up to the guys who needed it. We then heard a hellfire missile being released and screeching as it went. One of the other PSG's (platoon sergeants) called it up and asked if that's what he heard. Just as he called it up we saw the camera go white from the explosion of the hellfire and the secondary explosion of the IED that the missile hit. My guys ended up stumbling onto an AQI (Al Qaeda in Iraq) house. A little later I caught a glimpse of three guys standing on a roof top, a block away from my guys on the ground so I called that grid up and another missile went flying. It hit the AQI house. When all was said and done, there in the house lay 15 dead AQI

10

with enough weapons to arm an army.

That wasn't something that provoked a change in me. I noticed a real change in me after the first time I stepped out of a M1114 up-armored Humvee. As I said, I was addicted and I wanted more and more... and I got it. I ended up doing at least two dozen patrols in that last 6 months I was there. On October 11, 2008, we went out on another mission. This was the same mission as the half dozen before it; same ways, same areas and same times. We were tasked with showing the Iraqi NP's (national police) how to do their jobs. We taught them how to do soft knocks and hard knocks, as well as Snap TCP's (traffic control point).

We went around placing posters and talking to locals when I noticed something at one location. As we stopped at this little shack where they sold newspapers, snacks and sodas, there was a house in the background where on a balcony overlooking us was this ugly, old lady glaring at us with a hate in her eyes that I had never seen. Right next to this shack, about 10 ft. off the ground, was a PVC pipe where I soon heard a low rumble and a feeling of uneasiness grew in my gut. A few seconds later a huge gush of water came shooting out of the pipe, covering my entire left side. Shit water is what it was. The lady who had been glaring at us then disappeared after she flushed her toilet on us, well me. That was the beginning of the worst day of my life.

After lunch, where I had to eat alone because of the smell, we went back out for a third time that day at an IP (Iraqi police) check point where the guys were just lounging around. We stopped to find out why and while I was pulling security I heard a loud explosion. Then suddenly I felt the concussion of the blast, or what I thought was a blast. It turned out to be a bullet crashing through my face, then my jaw and out of my neck. It took no time at all for me to come back to reality when I heard the calmest and most trusting voice I had ever heard. The voice told me to put my hand on my neck and apply pressure (understand there was nobody around me and my mic had been destroyed by the bullet passing through it), so I did and made my way to cover. When I was behind cover, I noticed my LT (lieutenant) duck-walking around. When he got close, I grabbed him and put him behind me so as to use myself as a human shield because I was uncertain of my fate. All I knew was I would be damned if my LT was going to be shot by this possible sniper, so as my Medic, Doc Madison, worked on my left side, I had my LT on my right using my shoulder to steady his weapon while I called out targets.

My buddies and I would joke about what we would do if we got shot and how we would act afterwards. I can tell you none of that happened after I was shot. I was willing to die for the freedoms of my own country and the men and women who stood by my side in combat, but I was also willing to die so that the people of Iraq could feel what we feel every day, the right of choice and freedom to do whatever we set our minds to. I hear people yelling and screaming about how we should have never gone into Iraq and how there were no weapons of mass destruction, but in my mind the Hussein family was just that. I believe we went in there to do a job and we did it. He needed to be removed from power and his sons needed to be removed from everything. When a nation is terrorized by such evil and lives with the constant fear that people will be snatched from their homes and tortured for fun... that's when we need to step in and help out the little guys. Yes, there were many things that went wrong and many things happened that should not have, but we went in for a reason and it was the right reason, just the wrong wording. To this day, I am willing to fight for reasons just like that and I am willing to give my life so that others may actually live. We have a small saying within our doctrines, defined by the U.S. Constitution, that all men are created equal and we all have the right to pursue happiness. I believe that every man, woman and child in this world should have these same rights. Being the greatest force on earth, we have the duty and the honor of giving them that right.

LOOKING FORWARD: NOTHING LIKE THE REAL THING

D. Alex Wilson

I have thought about how I would write this essay dozens of times and have reconstructed how I would start it almost as much. Should I lace the piece with metaphors and comparisons, or should I try to relate the experience to something more common so that someone who has not actually gone through Post-Traumatic Stress Disorder (PTSD) or "combat stress" could attempt to understand? Or, should I just give a personal account of what happened to me and let people take from it what they may? In the end, I have decided to do a bit of all three in an attempt to convey two general themes:

1. There is nothing like the real thing with respect to life's many experiences, including PTSD, and
2. There is very low utility in looking back and reliving past bad experiences, except to learn from them and realize how they have shaped your life.

PTSD: Preparing for the Experience

"Life is a succession of lessons which must be lived to be understood" – Ralph Waldo Emerson

Combat stress/PTSD, like many other experiences in life, can be prepared for, but cannot be fully understood until that experience is actually felt and undergone. Innumerable experiences throughout life fit this description from sky diving to world travel to more personal things like going through puberty or having sex. And like sex, combat stress is an experience that has been a subject of popular culture, especially with regard to recent feature films.[1] Contemporary movies such

---

[1] During revisions of this essay, I reread this statement and was reminded of something my grandfather used to say often when my brothers and I were growing up. He lamented our TV (and movie)

as *American Sniper, The Hurt Locker, Fort Bliss, the Jason Bourne Series, Brothers* (2009) and *Man Down* (2015), to name just a few, show how PTSD can affect individuals' decisions with respect to their actions on the job (or in the military), as well as at home. Once they no longer have the ability to immerse themselves in the experience of war, the victims of PTSD portrayed in these films are no longer able to bury their feelings and smother their introspection.[2]

Many contemporary television programs also show the struggle with PTSD at various levels, ranging from smaller plot developments of supporting characters (Masterpiece Classic's *Mr. Selfridge*, ABC's *Grey's Anatomy*) to plot-dominating influences of main characters (Showtime's *Homeland* or Starz's *Banshee*). Writers and directors try to put the audience in the moment and make them feel like they know what it is to undergo that experience. In this way, the portrayal of combat

---

watching and restricted it when he was around because there was always "too much sex and violence" in those mediums; which, coincidentally is exactly what we are talking about here – the comparison of and relationship between sex and violence. One could even argue that there is a glorification of both sex and violence in our current society and whether that is right or wrong; but that is a topic for a different essay.

[2] As a very long aside, One very entertaining and underrated movie, in my opinion, is *The Hunted,* starring Benicio Del Toro and Tommy Lee Jones. This was potentially the first movie that I saw (though surely not the first one made) that depicts combat stress and the effects it can have. In the film, Jones plays a former military consultant, who, although never serving in the military himself or ever taking a life, has spent his career training elite operatives to do just that. Del Toro plays SFC Hallam, a former student of Jones' character, a PTSD-affected soldier who attempts to leave his former life of military service by hiding from the world in the woods. However, as Hallam knows too many secrets from too many missions, his former organization attempts to capture or kill him to keep the details of these missions from ever coming to light. In the end, Jones is forced to kill Hallam, who is in perpetual flight from the authorities, from his former organization, and most of all, from himself. Hallam continues to run and cannot stop, as, when he does halt and has time to reflect, he must confront and thus be haunted by all of the atrocities that he has witnessed and personally committed.

stress/PTSD symptoms is similar/parallel to how sex is often portrayed in popular culture, in the sense that you are expected to be transported to this experience so you can "feel" it without actually having gone through it yourself. But, however good the portrayal of the pain and loss of PTSD and the problems it can cause, viewing it is not realistically comparable to experiencing it yourself.

I would argue that for both of these life experiences – PTSD and sex – people can try to tell you what it is like and how it can affect you, but could never accurately portray either. Clinics proffer those clear plastic shelves stocked with poorly photocopied pamphlets entitled "Sex and You: Making the Most of Your Experience", or "PTSD and You: Making the Most of Your Experience", or "Cancer and You: Making the Most of Your Experience" or any other potentially stressful life experience for that matter. But these cannot accurately convey the event itself. People can relate their stories and tell you how to cope; you can prepare and think about it, and worry, and tell yourself that you are strong and you will perform flawlessly when going through it. But nothing you think, hear or read can ever compare to the experience itself. Nothing is like sex, except it. And nothing is like combat stress, or PTSD, or whatever one may label it as, except it. Until you have that nagging in the back of your mind to do something outside of (your former) character or you are paralyzed by a memory of the past, until you follow a safety procedure that is critical in wartime but superfluous, or even dangerous, in normal life, or until you have a recurring dream of an event or a decision made (or unmade) that perpetually haunts you...until then, you just cannot know what it is like.
I don't want to imply that someone who has experienced PTSD is any better or worse than anyone who hasn't. That is simply not the case. What I am saying is, simply, that it is a unique experience and makes true the cliché that "nothing is like the real thing." This creates a difficult situation, though, because the people who know something about it can't really describe it even if they wanted to do so. But—unlike sex—most don't even want to try relate it to others.

<u>PTSD: The Experience Begins</u>
"Given the choice between the experience of pain and nothing, I would choose pain."
– William Faulkner (from "The Wild Palms")

For me, what one could call combat stress or PTSD, has come in different forms. In general, I do not talk about my negative experiences often and try to refrain from talking about the stressful experiences I have had. It's a choice I've made: I don't want these experiences to be the defining points of my life, or the defining characteristics of myself in the eyes of others. Moreover, I have never, to my recollection, referred to combat stress/PTSD when talking about these events in my life. I was hesitant to even write this essay for the simple fact that I do not really think of myself and the difficulties that I have faced in that way. Although, I have received serious and permanent physical injuries from my time in the Army, the emotional and mental impacts of my experiences have been relatively minor (or at least that is what I have told myself over the past decade). I did, however, promise to include a personal perspective in this essay. Thus, I will try to walk the line of discretion and openness in order to convey some of what I was thinking at the time of my injury and recovery and how some negative incidents that occurred during my deployment have influenced me over the course of the last few years.

I have experienced several incidents which could have contributed to this sense of combat stress. Most were of a routine nature and did not leave lasting or memorable effects, although they may have contributed to my stress level in a cumulative fashion. However, I will touch on two experiences that have had lasting impressions on me, and not entirely for the worse. The first caused some serious stress at the time. The second experience occurred several months later and has greatly affected my life ever since.

The Unexpected Wakeup
On the evening in question, I was asleep in my trailer. At the time, I was performing the role of an assistant operations officer and was one of two individuals in charge of the Tactical Operations Center (TOC) for my unit. It was about ten minutes

16

before I normally woke up, and since I was perpetually exhausted, I never, ever, woke early.[3] That night, however, I woke up early and what's more, I woke up on the floor. I assumed I was so tired that I just rolled onto the floor at some point and had not stirred when it happened (which had occurred a few times before). And, as sleep was so precious, I just got back in bed until my alarm(s) went off.[4]

After my quick prep routine for the day, I walked outside of my trailer to see a large group of people in the road about 15 feet away from where I slept. After inquiring about what was going on, one of the bystanders said, "Man, you didn't hear that?" Apparently, a 75-mm rocket had landed right there in the middle of the road, had very fortunately *not* exploded, but hit so hard it was stuck in the ground (it was underground really). Eventually, I believe they blew it in place as they could not remove the rocket safely. Given my tiredness and my rush to get to the TOC, I don't remember thinking about it much at first. However, after I had time to ponder it, really think about it and what could have happened, I began to get this deep pit in my stomach. I tried to call someone to discuss it back home, but didn't get the opportunity to relate what happened. Even though there were some force protection measures in the vicinity, the rocket had a several hundred meter "blast radius" and was so close that I would have had a bad night, to say the least, if it had gone off. I still think about that incident often.

The IED (Improvised Explosive Device)
I will try to not to go too deep into the incident itself, instead attempting to discuss mainly the consequences.[5] As a

---

[3] I had three alarm clocks to make sure that I would wake up on time. Somewhat redundant, I agree, but as electricity was spotty, I always had an analog backup and I had another alarm clock on the other side of the room to make sure that I didn't just turn off my first two alarms in a stupor and fall back asleep.

[4] Funny story: At least once, when in high school, during football season, I was so tired that I fell from the top bed of the bunk-bed set in my room to the floor and still didn't wake up. Apparently, I used to be a very heavy sleeper, although I no longer am.

[5] I am not ashamed about what happened or about my service in

summary, however, one night as a platoon leader, I took one of my sections on a presence patrol in the town where we lived and conducted our operations. It was a mission that I had chosen (i.e., wasn't directly assigned) and I had planned (people, route, etc.). Towards the end of the mission, one of my Soldiers radioed and asked if I wanted to go back to our forward base. The road we were about to cross, that was the most immediate route home, had a very large IED (improvised explosive device) explode only a few days before. Further, I couldn't remember ever (or at least for a significant amount of time) driving on the road we were already on any further than we had that night, and I wanted to extend our presence to that neighborhood. For these and other reasons, I decided to go another block or two on our current route before going back. Thus, at this intersection while on this particular patrol, I had the choice of turning north and returning to base, or continuing east and continuing the mission. I chose the latter.

Before reaching the next main north/south road, an explosion went off. We had triggered a pressure plate victim-operated improvised explosive device (VOIED). The vehicle I was in was disabled on the spot and I was critically wounded. While returning fire, my team helped me to get back to base. I was immediately flown to Baghdad where I had the first of many surgeries. When I woke up over 14 hours later, my right leg was being held together by an external fixator and my left foot and ankle had been amputated.[6] After a few more stops and several surgeries, I finally arrived in San Antonio, Texas, where I completed my formal rehabilitation at the Center for the Intrepid (CFI).

---

general, nor is my injury and the way it happened a secret, I have just decided not to include a very detailed account here. It has, however, already been written about a few times, most notably by a writer named E.B. Boyd, who interviewed me on several occasions for a piece in my undergraduate alumni newspaper. It is the fullest and most faithful account out there, to my knowledge.

[6] I had an external fixator on my right leg to deal with a broken tibia (and fibula) and a below-the-knee transtibial amputation on my left leg.

At first, it was difficult to deal with what happened to me. For months, in the hospital and afterwards, I said to myself or dreamt the statement, "Should have gone North!... Should have gone North!... Should have gone North!" I relived the accident over and over and over again. I had an overwhelming need for justice which included a drive to find whomever had done this to me. I also often blamed myself because I was the patrol leader: every decision that brought me to that point (including having the mission at all) had been made by me. I exhibited unwarranted anger and irascibility directed at those I loved. I was nervous riding in the front passenger seat of a car and continually looked for bombs in the road and snipers on roofs. I lamented my now forever-changed life and the athlete that I could no longer be. I was changed by these negative thoughts and actions.

Eventually, I was able get over most of these behaviors, but I am still affected by some. And, as I said previously, not all of these "bad" experiences have affected me for the worse. In addition to personal development, which I will describe later in this essay, my outlook has changed with respect to doing and experiencing things now (within limits) instead of always putting them off. And, while it may seem strange, I now have the ability to pinpoint what literally was the worst moment/time in my life, at least from a personal aspect. I find comfort in being able to know what the absolute worst moment of my life has been; it affords me perspective whenever something bad happens or when I fear something bad is going to happen. And, hopefully, I will never have to lower that bar.

PTSD: A New Path[7]
>"*When a thing is done, it's done. Don't look back. Look forward to your next objective.*"
>*– General George C. Marshall*
>"*Even if you fall on your face, you're still moving forward.*" *–
>Victor Kiam*

---

[7] I wanted to subtitle it, 'A New Hope', but didn't want to take the thunder away from one of my favorite movies.

The methods that the physical therapists employed really helped me to get better both physically and mentally. My therapists[8] set up a series of challenges for me, as they did for many other injured service members to give us something to work towards. The first one that I signed up for was the MS150[9], a 150-mile bike race from San Antonio to the coast in Corpus Christi, Texas.[10] When my primary therapist told me about it on my first or second week of recovery my response was, "Don't you think that is a little far?" And, it was. But, the purpose of the race was not the race itself, it was the fact that I was working towards something: I had a goal, a purpose. Now, when I reflect on it, that period of training was my first step in the right direction. With a goal, however seemingly unachievable at the outset, I was able to reach out and make a start. I was able to move forward instead of continuing to stagnate. I began to get better physically and that allowed me to open up and get better mentally. I ended up completing about 127 miles of that race – 102 miles on a hand bike and 25 miles on a regular bike – which was a big achievement for me as I had only received my first prosthetic leg a week or two before the race. Through challenges like this and others (mini-triathlons, the Bataan Memorial Death March, etc.), the patients were able to work towards milestones, that, when achieved, allowed us to experience concrete progress towards rehabilitation.

Again, with this betterment of the self in a physical sense came

---

[8] I don't want to call anyone out here as I haven't asked anyone for permission to use their name, nor would I imagine they would want to be named. I think most therapists prefer to help from the background and take pleasure and pride in their work of helping others. That being said, I am grateful to all those who worked with me during my hospital stays, my recovery time in San Antonio, and afterwards. I quite literally would not be here without you.

[9] For more information: http://main.nationalmssociety.org/site/TR/Bike/TXHBikeEvents?pg=entry&fr_id=27923. The name has changed a bit but the cause is the same.

[10] Thanks also to Operation Comfort and all the other organizations and volunteers that helped with this and other recovery activities.

the betterment of the self in an emotional and mental sense. I think sometimes that Americans in general and people as a whole make themselves so busy that they rarely have time for reflection and introspection. One of the things that I liked most about my rehab was that I was allowed the time and opportunity to reflect on my situation – why I was where I was, and how I was going to progress forwards. This introspection in a safe environment, combined with the fact that I was working alongside others who were going through similar (and often more difficult) experiences, allowed me to put my new situation into perspective and keep a positive outlook despite the negative experiences I had endured. I didn't know what my life would be going forward, but I started to recognize the change in my life's path from how I had originally envisioned it.

Take one example:
One of the Wounded Warrior trips at the CFI took place in November 2007, shortly after the MS150 race in San Antonio.[11] The purpose was to explore west Texas, visit historical sites and continue to ride our bicycles to sustain our physical rehabilitation (I stuck to the hand bike). During one of our stops in Big Bend National Park, I was sitting on a wall overlooking a beautiful valley below, listening to music, writing in a journal and more or less just taking in the scenery. It was very early morning as I had trouble sleeping the previous night due to phantom pains[12] and suddenly I had the urge to follow the valley down to see if I could find a creek or stream below. Instinctively, I went to jump off the ledge, which was only about 6-8 feet off the ground below. At the last second, I performed a

---

[11] Again, Operation Comfort was a/the chief sponsor of this great event.

[12] My definition of phantom pain is simply the name given to the feeling that remains after an appendage is removed. It can manifest as actual pain (someone hammering a nail into your foot) or as often for me, like pins and needles (i.e., your foot is asleep). Based on a quick web search, for more information see:
http://www.mayoclinic.org/diseases-conditions/phantom-pain/basics/definition/con-20023268 or
http://www.ncbi.nlm.nih.gov/pmc/articles/PMC3198614/ or
http://bja.oxfordjournals.org/content/87/1/107.full.

very ungraceful twisting maneuver to grab the ledge before I fell completely, and I just as ungracefully pulled myself up (more like flopped) in order to find a spot where it was a bit easier to get down.

In the past, I would not have thought twice about jumping from that height and continuing on. Now I was afraid to even try. Granted, I think I had only been walking less than a month, but a total lack of knowledge of my new limitations and abilities stopped me from jumping. I had grown up an athlete[13], and suddenly at 26 years old, I didn't know my own capabilities anymore. Over nine years later, I can still remember and relive the confusion and overwhelming hesitancy I felt. Although, I had thought about it ad nauseam, this was finally the first time that I subconsciously and consciously accepted that my life would never be as it was; to face the fact that I was always and forever to be a different person (at least physically). I wouldn't really say that I began to feel limitations in a negative sense, or conversely that I was fully "OK" with my new status quo, but I did begin to change and accept this new version of myself. In a sense, acceptance became finding that easier way down to the valley; knowing that there were places I still wanted to go, but that I simply needed to find new ways of getting there.

PTSD and Snowboarding: The Future, Immediate and Otherwise

"Never look backwards or you'll fall down the stairs." – Rudyard
Kipling

One of my favorite pastimes in the world is snowboarding. It can, however, be quite a dangerous sport. The things you have to concentrate on are many: the surfaces of the board and the snow, your boarding partner, the temperature, the people who inevitably get in your way, the speed you are going and the fear of it, your muscle movements, fatigue, and the path ahead. With all of this to consider, there are at least two things that happen. One, you often have a hard time thinking of much else

---

[13] I played sports year-round during high school, football and rugby at the university level, and rugby while I was in the Army (but not for the Army team).

22

besides getting down the mountain safely. And two, you cannot look back. Sometimes you can glance back to make sure no one is going to catch up to you and run you over. Or, if you are in the lead, that your partner is close by and safe. But what you cannot do is focus all your attention on the path that is behind you. Any more than a fleeting glance backwards up the hill and you are bound to fall. Whether it is a minor obstacle like a small build-up of snow or an ice patch, or a major one like a large rock or a stout tree; something will always get in your way. Unless you are looking forward, you will fail. If you aren't, you might end up with a minor scrape or bruise or nothing at all. Then again, you might run head-on into a tree at thirty miles an hour.

Just like snowboarding, I believe that in life you cannot look back so long that it causes you to miss the present or the future. PTSD can be the force that causes you to reflect on what has happened to you and stop you from capitalizing on a great opportunity or a new relationship or just a chance to do something you have never done before. PTSD can slow you down, so much so that you don't see what is in front of you, only what has come before. Because PTSD is continually tempting you to look back and not forward, it may cause you to not see or be prepared for the other challenges and obstacles of life that you will inevitably face and must overcome. Instead of navigating around that figurative tree or over that patch of ice, you will trip up and fall. By looking back, you will also miss the simple enjoyment of going fast down the mountain of life itself. The obstacles created by PTSD can be large or small, mildly nagging or ever-present. It can manifest as a cyclical thing remembered on a certain day or a constant, perceptible, pervasive, all-encompassing evil. It can hinder you by changing your mood and causing you to be uncivil to others or yourself. It can cause you to be unable to think of anything else, to interact, or to work. For some, PTSD can be so bad that it transcends being the vehicle that causes obstacles to get in your way, but becomes that obstacle itself. It can be an ever-present hurdle – so high it can seem impossible to overcome. And, when it reaches this stage, what seems insurmountable can tragically lead some to take their own life.

23

Some people can concentrate on other things – like work, or travelling, or reading, or exercising – but none of these can be a permanent solution. No one can work indefinitely, no one can exercise constantly. No one, absolutely no one, can escape and run away from the past forever. But, with help, what they can do is face their fears, their consciences or their past experiences. Like snowboarders, PTSD suffers can and must look forward instead of backward. They can concentrate on what they are doing instead of what they did or what happened to them. If they do that, then they *may* get better. Unfortunately, some will not ever really "get better" or fully "be normal"; but, they can try. And, we can and must support their attempts to do so.

<u>*PTSD – Some General Thoughts*</u>:

"When people talk, listen completely. Most people never listen." –
Ernest Hemingway
I wanted to conclude with a list of some truths about combat stress/PTSD, at least for me:

- ***PTSD can be cyclical.*** Most of the things that used to affect me that may (or may not) be termed PTSD, no longer have the same effect. However, I do vividly remember and often think about my IED incident, most notably around the time of year of my injury. A week or so before, I begin thinking and dreaming about it more than I normally would. This continues until after the date of the accident.

- ***Dealing is different for everyone.*** Everyone has had different experiences and people deal with those experiences in different ways. Despite these varied experiences, most people I have met and talked to have had similar thoughts of "why me?" or "why now?" or "who is responsible?". Some people like to take it head-on, some take time to process what has occurred, while some take a very long time to accept their situation. Depending on their experiences and their character, some try to pretend that nothing is wrong, that nothing has really happened, or that nothing has really changed.

Although everyone deals with their specific situation in their own specific way, all must reflect and usually need to talk about their experiences in order to come to terms with them and get better. In fact, I have found that sharing one's experiences, especially with those you care about or with those who have had similar events in their lives, allows one to process these thoughts and feelings, and, in the end, improve.

- *Empathizing can be beneficial but don't overdo it.*
  What does PTSD mean for people who don't have it? Can they sympathize? Sure. Can they *empathize*? I don't know; but it doesn't hurt to try, if done correctly. Empathizing can be productive if done thoughtfully. But don't try to compare on equal terms your operation due to tennis elbow to someone who had their hand blown off. It might seem like you are trying to put yourself in their shoes, but this approach tends to come off as, at best, condescending, and at worst, fully disconnected and exceedingly diminishing. In essence, you would be doing the opposite of empathizing. Please, don't do this. For instance, I once had someone compare their nagging knee sprain from flag football to the surgery where I had a titanium rod put into my right tibia for stabilization and regrowth (as I had a significant gap between both sides of the break). This surgery involved pulling back the kneecap and hammering the rod through my bone (which was in several pieces at the time), then stabilizing the bone and the rod with screws. Although absolutely necessary for me to ever walk again, due to the newness and invasiveness of procedure, it actually hurt worse than the original injury to the leg (or the amputation on the other leg for that matter). The comparison left me speechless and made me feel like this person obviously had no idea what I was going through. So, again... don't do that.

  What can you do? Try simply thanking them for their service, or asking them how they are. I personally always prefer someone to ask me what happened, as opposed to just outright staring at my prosthetic leg and other injuries (or worse, hopelessly pretending not to stare). In fact, I always get nervous and self-conscious in the Spring when I start wearing shorts for the first time in months, as people tend to not-so-politely (or covertly) stare at me. Truly, just being straightforward about recognizing the existence of a lost limb or any other type of physical or mental injury is generally the best approach; staring is not.

- *More people are better than fewer.* During my recovery, I was fortunate enough to often have one of my friends or family members with me, especially at the beginning. At times, this could seem a bit oppressive as I sometimes tried to look good, be brave, or fight for them; but, eventually, I realized that I really just needed to fight for myself. Unquestionably, I did better with them than I would have without them. And, although I don't remember talking about my accident in detail with any of them, just their presence provided a degree of comfort that was instrumental to my recovery. My impression is that people with this type of support tend to do better than those without it.[14]

- *Time heals all wounds (at least a little bit).* Although "time heals all wounds" is another cliché, it can be true. For me, I found that behaviors like concentrating on the things that matter, recognizing where things have gone wrong in oneself, coming up with a plan to make them right, and forcing oneself to focus on the future instead of the past, have taken time to take root but have also gotten easier over time. The more time passes, the more some bad things fade (or at least their pull on you fades). Who knows, maybe one day nothing from that time will ever affect me again. I

---

[14] I am eternally grateful to everyone who flew or drove down to Texas to sit by my side and support me, if only to play video games, and the countless others who made gifts or donations to help. Thank you.

honestly don't think that will happen, but it may well be the case in the end.

Eradication of PTSD: T-minus...Never.

"I am not what happened to me, I am what I choose to become."
– Carl Gustav Jung

Finally, is it possible to completely eradicate PTSD from someone who has had it? I don't know, but for most, I doubt it. You cannot stop yourself from thoughts of the past, and some marks left on the body or in the psyche are permanent, but can be lessened with effort and time. Truly, time, reflection, and being straightforward with your path and your feelings, in my experience, can make it bearable. In time, it will hopefully seem more and more like a memory than real life. A bad experience, maybe, but nothing to fear. You may still lose sleep, you may never totally get over your own type of PTSD, and you certainly will never forget. But you can make it better.

My life changed drastically in 2007, but this May will be 10 years since that one time when I could have gone 'home' by turning north, but made the fateful decision to continue east, driving on until that VOIED went off beneath us. Since my injury, I've learned to scuba dive and kayak, and re-learned how to play sports, and do most of the things I could before, if just a bit differently. I've traveled to places I'd always wanted to visit but had only read about, and perhaps most importantly of all, I've taken chances that I would have been too afraid to take before or would have just pushed off to a more convenient time. For example, three months ago, I went on a bungee swing (a free fall of some 200 meters), something I probably would not have done before my injury. The guys that worked at the adventure park were great about my leg and helped me to face my fears, and I was able to do it, despite my injuries.

My journey has at times been challenging, but has included many great moments as well. I still think about and remember some of the bad experiences in my life, but through the help of others, I've been able to live and thrive in this new part of my life while always attempting to look to the future, instead of perpetually reliving the past. I believe that if you can do this, then you can focus on living those other experiences in life that you can read about but that you cannot really understand until you have done them yourself. Like bungee jumping or traveling or sex or snowboarding, just to name a few.

WE'RE NOT VICTIMS

Joshua Luke

We often turn on the TV and are bombarded with something regarding veterans. This was clearly highlighted in the 2016 election cycle, as everyone believed that they could secure the veteran vote under the notion that the veteran population can be lumped into a single group for voting purposes. In addition to this gross oversimplification of the entire veteran population, the media constantly paints a narrative of the Veteran who is suffering due to their service to the country. If there is anything that needs to happen in the veteran community, it is that the narrative has to be changed at every level. I was lucky enough that in my 9 years of active duty service in the Army, three years and three months of which were spent on various deployments, that I made it home safe and sound. For that, I will always be thankful, because I know people who weren't so lucky. That being said, I know many more veterans in my shoes than those who ended up paying a higher price for their service. As a veteran community, there appears to be the constant stigma of being "broken" because of our service. Many people approach veterans with a certain sympathy that should not be allowed to define the veteran community. Though the veteran community should not be defined as a "victim" population, we must also realize that some who come home are dealing with the repercussions of everything they've given for this country. The narrative behind PTSD has always held a stigma of weakness and mental health problems, which not only impedes a person's willingness to seek help, but also impacts the veteran at a very personal level. The military often attracts and promotes the strong-willed alpha personality, and the stigma of weakness can be as hard to deal with as the problems they bring home and face following deployment. The narrative within the Veteran community has to change if we are ever going to start making positive changes to the problems that exist.

To best understand misconception of the American

Veteran, it is essential that we examine the impact that service has on a person. Everyone understands the immediate sacrifice that is made by service members who volunteer to stand up and defend the United States in any way they are asked. This leads to grand patriotic thoughts and feelings by those who put on the uniform every day, as that patriotism is one of the mechanisms that is used to not only train military members, but also a method of accepting the harder situations that military life brings. One of the biggest lessons I learned while I served was that, though patriotism is an extremely important aspect of military life, there is a fine line between patriotism and nationalism; a line that is drawn in the sand by education and experience. There are no people who have a better understanding of what this means than those who have had the experience of seeing what type of impact political decisions regarding foreign policy have on the ground in the areas they affect. Veterans are the people who also understand the true cost of patriotism on both the sacrifice the country asked them to make and the people who have to live a life standing between sight posts of an assault rifle. There is a significant amount of very emotional discussions happening right now in the political world about foreign policy and whether it is the far right who spend much of their day fear mongering or the far left exploiting the saddest situations they can find in the world to pull at the heartstrings of their base. The discussion is always designed to manipulate the general population. With the frequency and operational tempo of military deployments over the last decade, the number of Veterans who have been able to personally get to know the people on the ground, who the media uses as a tool to push their agenda, is growing on a daily basis.

Not only does the military provide a hands-on foreign policy experience that very few other life choices will ever provide, but it also teaches a much more important lesson that unfortunately is often overlooked. In the military, regardless of branch of service, one of the very first lessons every Veteran learns is that personal actions do not just impact you. I do not know a Veteran who was never punished due to someone else's mistakes while they were in the service. This is an action that is very heavily criticized now-a-days in any other environment.

Yet, it was extremely good at instilling the importance of teamwork and brotherhood, or sisterhood as the family ties that service members make are co-ed, that really connects a military unit. A secondary impact of this style of training and unit building is really teaching the importance of civic responsibility. Veterans understand that decisions they make either in the civic arena or within their employment are going to impact others in their company or community. Given the current state of affairs in this country, the Veteran community understands, better than most, the importance of civic responsibility because they know that sometimes personal sacrifice is necessary for the bettering of the community. Many people feel entitled to the freedoms and rights that are given to the citizens of this country, but Veterans understand what the costs of these freedoms truly are. There is a quote that I have always felt epitomized how Americans feel about their freedoms and democracy...

"Everyone wants to go to heaven, but nobody wants to die."

This is the reality of democracy, as well as heaven. Though military service is not the only way to become a more complete citizen, it does provide experience that is very hard to duplicate in any other way. On top of this experience and understanding of the costs of freedom and democracy that military service provides, Veterans have already taken a significant step in proving they are committed to the protection of American values and willing to do what has to be done, at any level, to ensure those values are continued.

As the Veteran narrative is written by many who have never served and have no concept of what that experience is truly like, we end up with situations where many people now associate the stereotypes of a strict and rigid military lifestyle with an inability to adapt to fluid environments. The actuality of the situation is very different from that thought process. The military, unlike many other sectors, strives to instill leadership abilities and provides opportunities to even the most junior soldier to advance and grow professionally throughout their career. Many units have mentoring programs to help foster an environment where new soldiers are encouraged to take on responsibility and receive adequate support from leaders who have already accomplished similar tasks. The type of leadership experience is very unique to the military and provides Veterans with a set of qualifications that will be extremely beneficial as they transition to civilian employment.

The leadership ability is really just the start of what the Veteran community should actually want its narrative to be. The ability to adapt to changing situations on the ground is the key to success in an operational environment and this is invaluable in an ever-expanding global, corporate world. Not only is the speed of technological change going to increase, but so will the ways in which business is done moving forward. In addition to this ability to adapt comes the strength and resolve that it takes to maintain oneself regardless of the stress level of a situation. The speed at which the world now moves often-times creates situations that are capable of escalating quickly out of control. It is extremely important in these high stress and often fluid situations to be able to process and react with the calm and matriculated mindset that Veterans bring to employers. From an operational environment perspective, it is generally regarded that initial reports from any situation can be inaccurate, at least in some part, and it takes a very steady and calm temperament to be able to accurately analyze these situations and provide beneficial feedback in order for the best decisions to be made. This experience with evolving operational environments also gives the Veteran community a great advantage in the world of innovation, as their perspective on situations will likely be very different than those who all have had the standard civilian college then work experience. This comes full circle though with the sense of team that often has been the backbone of the Veteran experience. The need to be able to work well as a team can have serious outcomes in an operational environment and Veterans have the experience and drive to always make any personality differences work as a team for the success of the mission. The combination of these traits and experiences makes the Veteran community an extremely powerful asset to any employer.

Though all of these things should be the narrative for the Veteran community, the unfortunate reality is that PTSD has been a black cloud that looms heavy over us all. The first key to combatting this issue is to remove the stigma of weakness that is often associated with PTSD and the concept that this is a mental health fault. As the military operates effectively at creating a sense of pride in self and country, it often creates a dynamic that is not conducive to seeking help when help is needed. The first thing that must be accepted is that the symptoms that get classified as PTSD are not a weakness in someone's mental state but rather a normal reaction to extraordinary events. This fact alone will help remove the stigma that prevents Veterans from seeking the help they need and deserve.

Many people have begun to look at some of the issues associated with PTSD as the moral injuries of war and if we look at what is being asked of today's soldiers, then this becomes a much more understandable concept. We are no longer fighting clearly defined wars where the enemy is easily identifiable and the rules of war are accepted and generally adhered to. During current conflicts, soldiers are placed in the position to both win the hearts and minds of the local population, as well as assault and destroy the enemy. Many times, both of these things need to happen under the same roof. This situation is extremely difficult as soldiers often get welcomed into the house of a family, break bread with that family, laugh with that family, play with the kids of that family, and later that night they have to kick in the door of that very same house and try to conceptualize the reality that they may actually have to kill one of those family members. In other situations, those families feed and house a soldier for an afternoon may also be murdered, often brutally, and left on display for the soldiers in that area to see. How does one win the hearts and minds when even a little bit of progress is met with such overt brutality? Those situations weigh heavy on the hearts of soldiers and without a positive outlet it will become a bigger, darker issue. Then even if that doesn't get to someone, today's battlefields have also become highly televised criminal investigations. A soldier, who may be 18 years old, must not only constantly fear for what waits on the other side of that hill or just inside the next door, but also is in constant fear of what the legal ramifications will be once they return home. This has led to a very popular saying in the military...

"I'd rather be tried by 12 than carried by 6."

As a society, how can we blur the lines of operational responsibilities, train someone to operate in a warzone for the accomplishment of the mission, then hold a microscope to see how they handle every decision they are placed in? These soldiers do not often get the privilege of being able to analyze a situation and say that they may face legal dilemmas if they were to take on a given mission. Instead they are thrust into situations and asked many times to risk their lives while having to constantly fear life in prison, or worse for one wrong move. These soldiers are not being put into calm environments where there is time to analyze and process things for long periods of time, but rather the boundaries of these encounters are marked by violence and the immanence of deadly force being used against them. We, as a nation, ask service members to put their lives on the line to go to war where they take all the risks and get to participate in none of the decision making. We should not add the responsibility and fear of legal litigation over every single action. Unfortunately, violence is a factor of war and if the use of violence is considered inappropriate in specific areas for whatever reason then maybe there needs to be some reconsideration as to the necessity of war. The men and women who fight and die for this country should not have the added stress of prosecution.

I know some people will argue that just because there is a war going on doesn't mean that there should be immunity for those who commit egregious acts of violence during war. Occurrences like the prisoner treatment at Abu Ghraib or the marines who were caught urinating on the dead bodies of enemy combatants are often the justification used by those people. Though I would not condone any act that clearly violates the Geneva Convention, which the military spends a lot of time ensuring that every service member understands, I also do not believe that we should be looking under a microscope to find violations in order to push prosecution. Both the wars in Iraq and Afghanistan were fought by some with such brutality that the average person wouldn't be able to watch a movie about it. Obviously, there is going to be the existence of violence and death involved in any war, but these service members often see much worse. During my time in Baghdad it was not uncommon to find out that people were decapitated in the streets overnight and that was the least gruesome thing that occurred. There was a specific situation that occurred while I was deployed that truly highlights the depravity of what our soldiers had to face even when they were "winning the hearts and minds." During a patrol, a squad came across a dead body of a woman on the street and upon investigating the scene, the soldiers found that she had her stomach cut open and a small child was killed and stuffed inside. There is no amount of training to prepare anyone of any age to deal with that kind of lack of humanity, let alone to endure that on a daily basis for months at a time, and then to repeat that multiple times. These are the situations that contribute to issues that service members have when they return and it is by no means a weakness in someone's mental ability. These are extraordinary situations that no one should have to deal with and after the mission is complete, it is important that everyone feel empowered to do what it takes to deal with this.

One of the significant issues that is often associated with PTSD is the staggering suicide rate among Veterans and as a result, raises the question about how we begin to address the situation. As the narrative of PTSD transitions into one that makes it acceptable to get help, the key to combating the suicide epidemic is treatment of the underlying causes, usually associated with PTSD, as early as possible. From my experience, it appears that most veterans make the decision to end their life in times of transition, whether this is an employment transition, relationship transition, or any life change. This is partially to do with the military mentality of a mission-focused lifestyle. Many people are able to return home, start lives and put every ounce of their focus into work and family, shutting off any thoughts or issues they may have in regard to their service. The problem with this coping mechanism is that when something changes in their life and they no longer have that distraction, the issues they had attempted to hide away come back to haunt them. We see that for many older Veterans, this sort of trauma comes back after retirement when they end up having more free time where their mind can wonder. It is much easier to be strong when you are surrounded by people. Yet, unfortunately for some Veterans, the hardest battles they have to fight, they face alone. Getting to these issues early will help ensure that during these transition periods Veterans are better able to cope and will prevent some of those who consider suicide to be their only option.

The narrative must be changed in order to better represented and empower the Veteran community. The skill-set and experience that a Veteran possesses is an asset both to employers and the community as a whole. Democracy is a concept that helps ensure the freedoms that we cherish as Americans are protected. Veterans not only volunteered to fight for those freedoms, but understand the broader concept of the greater good of the community. This is the true value of the American Veteran and in order for them to continue to be the able to provide for this nation at any level we must create an environment in which they can receive the help they need after going through traumatic experiences. This will only become the case once the stigma over mental health is removed and we are able to accept that these are truly difficult situations in which we have asked them to operate. They have often dealt with things that are outside the realm of normal human behavior and thus their reactions are not a result of weakness but rather just a normal end state from having to deal with extraordinary situations. Nothing about these issues implies that someone is broken, and the Veteran community as a whole has so much more to offer than this stigma.

TOO YOUNG TO DIE

Brandon Tennery

I was born in Tulsa, Oklahoma, in December 1989, and then moved to Houston, Texas, shortly after birth. It wasn't long before I moved again to League City, Texas to be with my grandfather, who happened to work for NASA. From a really young age, baseball became everything to me. The great thing about Texas is that you can play baseball all year round. From spring ball, fall ball, travel teams and all-star teams. Though I played other sports as well, baseball just had my heart from a young age as it still does today. After fooling around in school too much, I was sent to a Job Corps in San Marcos, Texas. After graduating at 16, I decided to make the move to better my life from the bad situation I had been around. I was then taken in by a pastor and his family in Dallas, Texas. A year later, I decided I was ready to fulfill my childhood dream and become a soldier in the United States Army.

In March 2008, I went to Basic Training and AIT (Advanced Individual Training). Upon my graduation, I moved to Colorado Springs, Colorado, where I was stationed at Fort Carson and assigned to the 4th Infantry Division, 4th Brigade Combat Team.

In March 2009, I received orders for my first tour to Eastern Afghanistan, where I was based out of a COP (Combat Outpost). After sustaining mild injuries on my that tour, my unit returned to Fort Carson, Colorado in June of 2010. After being promoted to Sergeant on my 21st birthday in December 2010, I was on top of the world. Shortly after my promotion in May 2011, I received orders to report to Fort Bliss in El Paso, Texas. After getting to my new unit in 1st Armored Division, 3rd Brigade, 4th Battalion, I was told to get ready to deploy again.

In August 2011, I returned to Afghanistan. I was now in a leadership position at 21, full of energy and ready to exceed the expectations of my unit. This deployment was again to a small COP in the middle of the mountains. We got attacked almost daily. Then the day of April 11th, 2012 happened.

At around 11:00am, our outpost started to take small arms fire with simultaneous mortar fire from all directions. I threw my vest on and grabbed my Kevlar while clutching my rifle tightly in my right hand. I rushed to the top of a hill so I could get to the high ground. Adrenaline was thriving with nothing on my mind but killing the enemy before they could kill one of us.

"Zzzzmp zzzmp zzzmp," enemy fire flew over us from all different directions.

I saw the rounds hitting and ricocheting off the mountain all around me. Following my lead were my teammates and soldiers. The last thing I remember before the blast was the horrible ringing in my ears and then silence with debris hitting all over my body and helmet. Upon catching up to me, my soldiers found me unconscious and having seizures. I was blown back several feet and slightly burned from two RPG (rocket-propelled grenade) blasts, and received a bullet to my vest. I would suffer from a severe traumatic brain injury, external wounds, internal wounds, slight loss of vision and hearing, as well as balance problems. I still have ongoing physical pain in my back, head and knees from the blasts. I now have a seizure disorder which alters most thing I do.

I owe my life to the medic and my fellow soldiers that did an amazing job getting me stabilized while risking their lives. They rendered immediate care, strapped me to a litter using their own belts to secure my body and then took me off that hill while still under fire. They stopped along the way to fire back at the enemy. The enemy started taking shots at the MEDEVAC Helicopter (medical evacuation transport) coming in to take me to FOB (forward operating base) Shank, where there was a field hospital. The pilots didn't have to come, but when they did, their gunner was on point and everyone was engaging the enemy so we could get out of there as soon as possible. I was still unconscious. Everyone that day had a part in saving me from dying. I'll never know the other people who helped me that day besides the guys right by my side. When I was transported to FOB Shank, my blood pressure rose to

261/158. I was intubated and a stent would be placed in my neck. They worked on me for a few hours before my body would be transferred to Bagram Air Field Hospital. I would later find out that the field Doctors paralyzed my body, because they couldn't do their job with me having multiple seizures. Only then were they able to work on me and my wounds.

During all that madness, I had an experience that everything my Grandfather had said was true. I dreamt that I woke up for what felt like only 20 seconds and there was a white sheet over my head. As I tried to raise my arm to take this cover off of my face, I couldn't. I thought I knew what was about to happen, so I asked my Grandfather, who was the biggest impact in my life and an evangelist that I had growing up, to come get me and take me with him to the eternal life I've read and heard about my whole life. He had passed away in 2006 and I think about him daily. I kept a picture of him and me in my left breast pocket over my heart on both deployments so that he would always be with me, watching over me and my team.

"Come get me and take me with you," I spoke to him.

I thought for sure in my heart I wasn't going to make it. I thought that was where it was going to end... in the middle of a shithole country at 21 years old. I closed my eyes, said a prayer and then in this experience I saw the most incredible sight I had ever seen. It was the brightest of lights I'd ever witnessed with his face just staring at me. In that moment, my Grandfather and I were together again. It was the most peaceful feeling I've ever experienced. We were right back at a spot at our campgrounds in Bandera, Texas. I can vividly remember everything about this experience from the smells, sounds and watching the sunset. I remember standing in the back of the tabernacle and the church camp I grew up going to that overlooked that beautiful sunset. It was a place my Grandfather and I cherished until the day he passed away.

I woke up feeling peaceful that my time wasn't up yet. Strangers seemed to be brothers and sisters in uniform that I could count on. I'll probably never see or meet those involved, but they had a part in a day I'll never forget.

39

I needed more extensive treatment, so I got sent to Germany for a couple of weeks before finally reaching the final destination at Brooke Army Medical Center (BAMMC/SAMMC) in San Antonio, Texas. There I continued my rehab for almost two years, going through multiple procedures and a few surgeries. Now, I have trouble with my speech and memory. I walk with a cane for when I have severe pain or after seizures. After rehab, I was assigned to the Warrior Transition Battalion full time at Fort Sam Houston in San Antonio, Texas.

I started competing in adaptive sports, speech therapy and made multiple trips to the TBI (traumatic brain injury) clinic, mental health and neurology to get me as close to normal as possible. While in the Warrior Transition Battalion, I started earning medals and ribbons for swimming and fencing. I then started getting my confidence back. Baseball is still my passion. I was told I wouldn't be able to play again and would have to limit my activities to almost zero. At the beginning of 2013, I was asked to play for the Army Purple Heart Baseball team. My childhood dreams were coming true. We played at Angels Stadium in Anaheim, California, facing the Marine Purple Heart Baseball team and beat them 20 to 9.

I still felt off, like an outcast of society. I was asked to speak at a church in front of the congregation. They had no idea what to think of me and I was really nervous as I started to sweat profusely. I lost my focus as my mind raced back to Afghanistan. The memories were so vivid and I felt like I was going to vomit. I then showed them pictures and clips of us being deployed. They just gave me a blank stare. One member even tried to relate what I did in Afghanistan to a fucking video game after the service ended. Seriously?

I know I'm not normal after going to war. It has forever left its mark on me and although my time at war is done, it will never mentally go away. My body, mind and soul will never be the same. However, the goal is to just work on it as much as possible. It takes time and for me it took a lot of drinking before I was really able to talk to anybody. I avoided family and friends because I was ashamed of myself. In my head, I was supposed to be this soldier and leader who came up from hard times, but always kept pushing forward. After getting out of the Army, I found myself not wanting to do anything and just stayed secluded. I was afraid of the world. I would wake up screaming and drenched in sweat while sometimes vomiting from my nightmares. There was a point I was afraid to even go to sleep. Since I was 18 though, it's all I've known. Until I became a part of Heroes Sports, playing the sport I love, and received that comradery I missed so much, I felt like I didn't have a place.

One minute I was in a war zone. The next minute I'm wounded and in hospitals getting flown from one location to another feeling confused and in pain, just wanting to get back to my soldiers. Now, I'm back in the States and in this crazy, fast paced world with new cell phones and technology. I couldn't even figure out how to use my phone again due to my head trauma. I'll tell you, it's a very rough adjustment. It takes time and it's not easy. I try to keep in contact with the men I was with. That helps keep me sane, but I never fully got back to normal.

The worst thing to hear from people is that you're different now.

No one wants to hear that. It's upsetting and makes you want to deny it even more, but deep inside, you can't fool yourself. We've all changed and will always be different. After being injured and joining the non-profit, Heroes Sports, I couldn't play baseball the same or even be out in the Sun and on the field too long. I seemed there wasn't a place on the ball field that I didn't throw up on from my brain and internal injuries. Of course, my teammates would give me shit, but I'd never leave the ball field. I just kept a little bottle of Listerine in my back-left pocket and kept pushing on. It turned into a superstition of mine after doing so well at our first baseball game. "Baseball Players..."

Painting and writing about moments in life is when I started to expand my mind. It helps me tap into my subconscious mind and release everything that I have trouble wanting to think or talk about. I have also realized my nightmares are not as bad when I paint that day. Some of the benefits of painting that I've found are that it helps the mind, soul and the things we hold inside that a lot of us cannot talk

41

about.

#PAINTHROUGHPAINT

  I now live in San Antonio, Texas with my incredible dog, Beau, who I received from Jeff Anderson at rebuildingwarriors.com. I plan to start going back to school to become a photo journalist at Texas Lutheran University. I continue playing sports, socializing and helping the community. I enjoy getting the comradery back with my teammates who are also Veterans with the Non-Profit organization, **HEROES SPORTS,** founded by **Mike Barker.** Writing has also helped me express my experiences, so I'll end this piece with a poem I wrote...

FACES
These Faces of sadness,
These Faces of shame,
The Faces of guilt, I hide behind my pain.
I don't want to face them because I know what comes next,
The memories come back, now there's vomit on my chest.
I wake up screaming, I just want to end it all.
And right after that I find myself hitting the wall.
The Face I show you, is the one I want you to see.
It's usually a happy one, just like I used to be.
So I smile and smile then put on this Face, even though I feel so
out of place
Everyone around me doesn't even know, that this internal war
I'll never let go.
I remember your face right before you died, so white and cold,
there's nowhere to hide.
As tears form up I quickly brush them aside.
I look at my men and just wonder why?
Their faces say it all, there's no need for words to be spoke,
He's just 19, this has to be a cruel joke.
I take one more glance at this young man's face, what a shame,
a fall from grace.
The only thing left is my reflection in his eyes.
Now let's go kill the Enemy.
All you hear are battle cries.

We'll avenge your death; I promise you that!
But until we meet again, I'll have to face the fact
That the Faces you see aren't always so real,
Because I have this pain inside that just won't heal.

PATROLLING FOR CLEMENCY

David Rogers

Every night I have this recurring dream. It has been for months, maybe years. I see the guys. We are all there and in our original form, from years ago. We are fuller and healthier looking, but we've been in the 'Stan (Afghanistan) for months now. Lack of food, lack of sleep, tattooed with grime and sun-blistered faces. We look exhausted, skinny and underfed. These were the conditions. Light chow when it was available, patrols nonstop, an unforgiving sun and bitterly cold nights.

In my dream, we have just gotten back from a patrol. We made contact with the enemy with sporadic gunfire. Nothing crazy or extravagant, at least not to us. Every day you fired at LEAST a couple rounds from your rifle. If you didn't, then something was wrong or the enemy was planning something big. Silence was eerie, and could translate to bad things, like a pending complex ambush around the next curve in the road. We file back inside the wire, peel our gear off and migrate to the side of the tents to have a smoke. Time seems to move slower. As we smoke, we reflect on the events of the firefight. We call each other out, making jokes of how one or some looked scared, froze up, tripped and fell, or looked totally "badass." We mimic the screams, the yells and the commands...

"C-c-c-contaaaact!"
"Where?!"
"God dammit, someone secure the flanking positions!"
"Call HQ and let them know we got this!"

It's funny to us. Our jokes are all in good fun and not actually putting anyone down. As the adrenaline subsides, we begin to shift the conversation to girls. All the girls we've fucked or almost fucked. All the girls we wanted to fuck and all the girls that are "bitches," because they wouldn't fuck us. Some of us have known each other for years. We replay stories of our attempts, failed attempts and wingman stories

45

supporting one another. We laugh at how drunk and stupid we were. "How in the hell did you even pull that off?" Someone cries, as they laugh. We begin to all laugh. We are dying; we are crying. It is such a happy time, despite the current situation. I have never been so fucking happy in my life. They say the less you have, the less you need. Whomever "they" are might actually be right. I think I might have wiped more tears from my face from laughing so hard during those days. Yea, lots of sad shit happened, but you compartmentalized and found solace in the smallest of happy things.

The dream. It still feels so real. The smells, the sounds, the aching of my abdomen from laughing so hard is still there. As the night grows colder and the seconds of time continue to tick into the future we are still there laughing, telling stories and enjoying each other's company. I finish my cigarette, pull out a fresh pack and begin to pack it. *Smack-smack-smack!* I systematically bounce the smokes off my hand. I tear into the package and pull one out. Before lighting it, I offer everyone another smoke. And, before I know it I'm down to six left in the pack (funny, how that always works. I don't mind it though. I know they'll give me one or four sometime in the future). As I draw in my first drag someone makes a funny comment and we all begin to chuckle. One of the guys throws out a "fuuuuuccckk you." As the giggles die down there is an awkward, strange, almost eerie silence. My buddy looks up to me with a serious face, his lips are half smirked.

He asks, "Why, bro? Why did you leave us?"

I'm studying his face trying to formulate an appropriate response and I'm in shock from the question. By now, everyone is dead silent and staring at me muttering a soft, multi-voiced, "Yea." Everyone's face is blankly honed in. They are all truly concerned and curious. What can I say? I came down on orders to a new duty station? I decided not to reenlist? Or, I was Honorably Discharged? The war has been over for me, but the war didn't end/stop there for everyone.

At this point, every time, it is as if my body or maybe my soul is sucked out of this scenario like a vacuum. As I am sucked back to reality, I whiz by assorted emotions and events from that time to present day. Then I wake up. My eyes jolt open, I regain consciousness and quickly realize it was only a dream. It is dark; my girlfriend Katie and my dog Bragg are sound asleep next to me. They are warm, I am safe, but am I really happy? Short answer, yes. In a more complex, difficult philosophical ponder... no.

I'm not sure who died then. Did I die or did they die? Or is this my subconscious telling me that those times are dead and to move on? Either way, I can't. I can't, because I don't want to. They are a piece of me. They helped shape and define the man I am today. To forget, to let go, to simply move on, to me, is disrespectful to them. I weep quietly in the night, as Katie and Bragg sleep. Sometimes, I think Bragg knows, so he scoots a little closer to me and cuddles up. I think he is trying to comfort me the best way he can. Words cannot heal that kind of sadness. He knows that, so he just lets me do what I need and subtlety lets me know he is there for me (I swear that dog knows me better than I know myself sometimes). You see, for some of us, they are still stuck there in time. For some of us the war just changed into new battles. For myself, the war turned psychological. I still fight in my head during a dinner party. I still fight during an interview. I still fight while sitting in class pretending to be an adjusted civilian-member of society. I'm always at war. Now, it's just with myself.

Nobody knows it, but I'm so haunted inside. I go to therapy, I take pills, but I can't share this kind of stuff. My therapist is so amazing and really wants to help me sort some of these things out, but I am still just not ready to share. Before I can share, I believe I have to make sense of it first. Find the answers. Maybe, that's why I write so much. If I write out my emotions enough times, maybe they will fall into place. Then I can dream of normal things like flying at tree-level, winning the lottery, etc. You know, the things normal people dream.

Call Sign: Raven

This concludes Chalk One.

RESUPPLY 1

In war, we occasionally need to stop, take a knee, drink water and then continue the mission.   The next two stories are a change of pace with unique perspectives. A wife and a Marine turned security contractor give you their stories.

EVERYTHING AND NOTHING
Amy Miner

Amy was the wife of a combat veteran. His burdens
became hers.

I lost the love of my life. Now I have to go downstairs. They are
waiting for me. While they wait, I stand in a room I don't want
to be in, but I never want to leave. I'm staring into a closet with
nothing to wear. No clothes for my new title. A title I do not
want.

*   *   *

I found a shirt. Black. Black pants. Black boots. Black
bra. Black underwear. Black socks. I'm running on autopilot
for a few minutes, and then I am focused. I walk over to the
oddly-placed sink in our bedroom and grab a q-tip. His q-tip.
He was obsessed with cleaning his ears. The ceramic container
was always full of the tiny cotton swabs. I hold one under a
light stream of water, just enough to get the tip wet but not
saturated. I get down on my hands and knees and crawl over to
him. I rub the damp q-tip in his dried blood. The only piece of
him left is soaked in the carpet, dry now. As the white cotton
tip starts to turn red, I begin to cry. I don't want to leave this
place. The only place he is. I'm frantic now. Crying, trying to
get all that's left of him onto the fucking end of a q-tip. In a
split-second I stop crying. I stand up, put the q-tip into my
jewelry box next to the earrings he bought me to replace the
ones he broke. I wipe my face, open the door and head down
the stairs to the new responsibilities I never wanted.

He was everything. We were each other's everything
from early in our relationship. We were a blind date that
turned into a friendship that turned into love. That first night,
we talked for hours about TV shows, music, traveling, life
experiences... everything. The innocence of an eighteen-year-

51

old girl that was just starting her life and a twenty-four-year-old guy who had lived so much already. We were just lost in each other. Enveloped by a bubble where the future didn't matter and what either of us experienced in the past no longer existed. This new friendship evolved into so much more with one question.

"Can I kiss you?"

With that one kiss, everything changed. One touch of his hand on my face, feeling his breath on my lips, leading up to the perfect kiss and that was it. All our plans changed in that moment. We just didn't know it yet.

People always talk about the outward signs of trouble. He had been to war prior to us meeting. It was a life I had never known and he showed no hint that it was a difficult life. Maybe then it wasn't. If only we could have seen what was to come. What the years of suppressing the things he had to do, the things he had seen, the life he had to live would do. How it would change him. The many "boxes" he would hide them away in would open unexpectedly, pouring out a memory or a feeling from a different life that was only a few years in the past. Having to take lives, losing friends, barging into homes where families lived. Pointing guns at children and women. Taking away fathers and brothers, all in the name of peace and safety.

Shortly after we met, he made the decision to leave active military life. He tried employment in the civilian world but would either lose his job or quit. We would joke about him leaving a job. He would say they never felt like the right fit. We didn't pick up that the difficulty in keeping a job was the difficulty associated with transitioning from military life, from death, from war to a "normal" life. After a few years, his behavior began to change, only becoming worse once he reenlisted into the Army National Guard and started government contracting. So much time was away from us. There were times we would only see each other for a total of six to eight weeks out of a year. More war, more death, more isolation. More of living in a world where every little thing he did could be life or death. The anger increased. The resentment, the drinking, the self-sabotage, the paranoia, the high-risk behavior, the affairs and the abuse started. When the boxes would open, he would ignore what was spilling out and turn to these negative and destructive behaviors.

We were a close family unit, the six of us. We were his unit. We had his back without question. I protected him with no regard for my own life. My life was his life. Soon, I gave up jobs that I loved so he could fulfill a void he was feeling. This helped to keep things calm. Over the years, we all learned how to conform to what he needed. We knew where we should sit in a restaurant so that he would be comfortable. I knew to avoid any kind of unknown object on the road while driving. I finally figured out the exact volume set (27) for the radio in the car if he fell asleep. This volume level allowed me to hear the music and muffle any noises coming from outside the car that could startle him awake. We knew how to read his mood within one minute of him walking in the door. There were nights I would wake to him asking, "Did you hear that?" In a flash, he would be out of bed, weapon in hand, clearing the house and securing the outside perimeter of our home. Sometimes it would take five minutes. Other times, it would go on for over an hour. I learned to take on his burdens as my own. It was the only way. Seeing the pain and confusion in his eyes was enough to fuel my need to never give up on him.

I knew he was still in there somewhere. Lost.

I've heard people say that PTSD puts distance between the sufferer and his or her loved ones. At times, I felt that way. I would ask myself who was lying next to me. How could he do and say these awful things to me one day and act like they never happened the next?

Other times I felt like the PTSD brought me into his world. Every minute of our life was consumed by this. I felt I needed to be in his world if I was ever going to be able to help him. No matter what we were doing or where we were, I was on high alert. If there was a slight change in him, I had to be ready. The change could be as subtle as his eye contact becoming more intense or how tightly he would start to hold a cup. Being able to detect these changes allowed me to

53

formulate a plan to de-escalate the situation. This wasn't something I wanted to do. This was a learned behavior on my part.

Slowly, over the years he told me everything. He told me about his work overseas, ALL the infidelities, the lies... everything. At first, it felt good to be completely in the loop. It was almost a relief to hear it all laid out. I wasn't crazy after all! And with this realization, I took on a new role... his "rock." I was the one that fixed everything. Found solutions to problems. Helped to clarify lies he told or participated in his lies to protect him from being portrayed a liar. Countless hours were spent talking about his needs, his feelings, his wants, his triggers. When I would try to talk to him about how I was affected by these things, it would turn into him calling himself a "piece of shit" which would steer the focus of the conversation back to him.

The shower became the place where everything was talked about. Nothing was off limits. At times, it reminded me of a confessional. This is where he would break down. The place he would cry and punch himself. We would sit there naked and he would bare his soul to me. Maybe he felt that if he told his "sins" to me they would be washed away with the water down the drain and he would be cleansed. I began to feel an overwhelming pressure to become the "rock" he thought I was. If I could just get him to see himself the way I saw him, maybe, just maybe he would be okay. These "shower sessions" became his release. Every day, sometimes twice a day, I would sit with him while he verbalized whatever thoughts were in his head. He would punish himself physically while I tried to stop him. I would let him know he was worth more than the things he did and said. Sometimes we would sit there until the water ran cold, but I never budged. He called these sessions and only he ended them. Although many of his actions would be unforgivable to most, I could understand the "whys." This does not mean that understanding him was a free pass. The things he had done and said hurt me to my core. They broke my heart. I only wanted to pull him out of the clutches of these demons, then I could have my partner, my equal, back.

I would constantly ask him to go to counseling. He finally went, but it was short-lived once he found out he could lose his security clearance and his job. So, he lied to the counselor saying he was leaving the area and ended counseling. He told me he was "red flagged" by the military, but he was able to give the right answers and persuade the right people to allow him to go overseas. They needed him just as much as he needed them. It was seemingly a win-win scenario to ignore the signs. He feared what his friends would think of him if he admitted he needed help.

I pleaded with him one night. I told him I couldn't be his wife and his counselor. He needed to understand the information he was telling me was difficult for me to hear because it involved me.

He lashed out and said, "You're the one who wanted to know, so you're the one who has to take it."

How could he expect me to be objective when he was confessing all his sins to me and treating me horribly when we were alone? I was the one he said "I love you" to and also the one who he took it all out on. This was when I learned to just be a face he talked to. A face who heard these confessions and forgave. Meanwhile, I lost myself and my self-worth.

When he was around, our children and I walked on eggshells. We learned every single trigger and let them drive our lives. We enjoyed the good moments, but knew they were fleeting and would come with consequences. The rage became worse and more hateful, while the apologies became fewer and emptier.

To this day, I still believe that you should never give up on someone you love. He was lost, but he let himself become so lost that by the time we knew what was happening, he was unreachable. He didn't ask for help when he began to have behavioral changes. He hid them, blamed others or made excuses. So many people looked up to him for so many different reasons and he feared letting them down or changing how they saw him. If he admitted he hated himself and the things he was doing, they would no longer look up to him. He felt like a failure and undeserving of the idolization by others that kept him going at times. It was easier for him to give into these destructive behaviors than to challenge his entire understanding of himself.

In his words, "These behaviors would be forgiven and accepted. Getting help wouldn't."

There were times I found myself becoming resentful of his friends. I began to shift blame to them. I felt that their acceptance of his behaviors only encouraged him to continue them. I would wonder how they couldn't see what I KNEW. But he gave them the fun, charismatic, "life of the party" friend. He didn't let them into his world. He gave them what he thought they wanted. He would come home exhausted and sad, feeling that if they knew what he really was, they would hate him. He became consumed with what others thought of him. His paranoia about what he believed they were saying about him led to an attempt on his own life and a very short stint at the VA (Veterans Affairs) hospital after a three-day stay in the local ER.

I fought for his release during those three days in the hopes he would get actual help with the VA. Once at the VA hospital, they did an intake and I left him there. I didn't cry until I was at the car. I cried because I felt like I had failed him. I cried because he was my best friend, the love of my life and I couldn't stay with him. I cried because I was relieved to finally have help.

Less than 18 hours later, my phone rang. They were releasing him. He said they told him he didn't require further inpatient care. I was on my way to get him. I was stunned. A veteran attempts to take his own life, sits in an ER for three days where he receives random visits from psychiatric doctors, does not receive any real intervention and waits for a bed at the VA hospital. Then when he finally gets to the VA, they decide in less than twenty-four hours that he doesn't need their help. He was referred to our local VA office for a follow-up. There was no appointment made. We had to show up at the site and wait. Finally, we were summoned into the office by a psychologist. We sat with the clinician. I was relieved, once again, to finally have someone intervening and able to help me care for him. He was relieved that someone was going to see he needed something.

We spent the first forty-five minutes talking about his suicide attempt and the last 10 minutes coming up with a safety plan for when we went home. We were told to come back tomorrow for another visit. We were not given an appointment, but told to show up at about the same time and we would be seen. The next day we returned and waited. Again, his name was called but it wasn't the woman we saw the day before. This was a new clinician. We sat with her and she told us about her experience helping combat veterans. After about ten minutes of listening to her resume, she finally turned her attention to my husband. She proceeded to tell us that she had read his file but wanted to hear in his own words what happened. Thirty minutes later, with only 5 minutes left in the session, she began to go over a safety plan. It was then that I interrupted her and explained that we had done all of that yesterday with someone else. I explained that my husband needed immediate help with coping mechanisms for working through his feelings of despair, rage, self-sabotage, emptiness, guilt, undeserving of a good life, emotional numbness and inability to stop what he does. She informed us we were out of time but treatment would get started next time. I was starting to feel like Dorothy in The Wizard of Oz... "Come back tomorrow and the wizard can help you!"

Day three. More waiting. Another clinician we had never met. Another resume. Then the same comment, "I read about what happened but I'd like to hear it from you." I was beyond pissed. With no other options, we had to continue. Another explanation in his words. Another safety plan.

Day four was finally new! A meeting with the medical director about what medications my husband might benefit from. I informed the psychiatrist that we were not there for medication. Nevertheless, he was prescribed a medication to help with sleep. After a few more sessions, over a few more weeks, we realized we were going to have to find an alternative to the VA.

I contacted the local Veteran center and my husband started counseling. We were connected with a therapist who was a "matter of fact" kind of guy with over 30 years of experience counseling vets. He saw the same counselor until his death. The same counselor helped me after my husband died. I still think of that counselor (who retired shortly after my husband's death) fondly. Although he was finally getting counseling, he continued to spiral out of control. He was hitting himself more, even giving himself a black eye. He was struggling every day with his self-worth. Thinking about what he had put the five of us through over the years overwhelmed him. He was seeing how he was unable to control his behaviors, his emotions and the fears that show themselves with PTSD. Good days were few and far between. Our "shower sessions" increased but he talked less. We finally had a community of support that was there for him. They knew the surface of what it was about. They knew about his PTSD. But they had no idea what we had all been through for years.

*   *   *

The second he let go of my hand while I drove the car that dark chilly night, I knew. Instantly, I went from the compassionate wife listening to her husband belittle and hit himself to the protective mother in need of keeping her four babies safe. I blocked out his hateful words as I drove. The names he was calling me. The threats he was making. In my mind, I was outlining which emergency plan to put in play this time. Which plan would calm him and distract him enough to keep the kids safe. With my mind going a million miles a minute, I pulled into the driveway. I told the kids to get out of the car as he punched the dashboard. I threw the keys to them as they ran inside. They knew the drill. We had done this too many times to count.

He was in a full rage. I hadn't been able to make eye contact with him while I was driving. He jumped out of the car, kicked the light post and hit the mailbox on his way up the porch steps. I sat for five seconds preparing for another de-escalation effort. I followed him up the stairs and into our bedroom. Finally, as he was yelling and threatening me, I saw his eyes. I couldn't see him anywhere in them. I tried every technique I had read about. I tried every plan I had ever used. None of it was working. Chaos ensued for what felt like eternity. Yelling, choking, more yelling. I knew I needed to get the kids out of the house. No matter what happened to me, they needed to be safe.

Gun shots.
Holding my child.
Trying to breathe life into the love of my life.
Holding my child who was forced to save us all.
Protecting my children.
Ignoring the police and taking my time to say goodbye.
Climbing onto his lifeless body and holding him.
Telling him I will love him.
Always.

The numbness and emptiness that stays with you after losing someone that should still be here is indescribable. This shouldn't have happened, but there was no other way. My husband was gone before the bullets entered him. I will never forget his eyes that night: empty and void of the man I knew for over twenty years. His fight ended and I have so many mixed feelings about his death. Why did he stop fighting? In some ways, I'm not sorry for his loss. I am sorry I couldn't save him from himself. This may sound harsh and the difference may be lost on many, but I hope they never have to know the difference. He left us with an emptiness that can never be filled. He left us alive, but having to start over. We now must carry on with mixed feelings when we think of him. How do you make a new life when you gave your life to someone who is now gone forever?

At the funeral parlor, everyone has left the room. It's just us. I'm kneeling over him and I can't leave. Times passes. In the gentlest voice I've ever heard, the director tells me it's time to go. I tell him I can't leave him. I'm crying. He asks if I need someone to come in. I ask him to send in my husband's close friend. His friend comes in. I tell him I can't leave my husband: he can't stay there by himself. He gently holds my shoulders and tells me we must go. I'm sobbing. I can hardly stand. He reasons with me, telling me that he's gone. This isn't the man I love, it's just his body. He is gone and not in the room. I cry and accept this. I look back at him one more time. I walk out.

I'm standing in the room staring at his lifeless body while my family, our children and a few very close friends surround us. The director walks from the casket to me. He hands me my husband's wedding ring and a pin that was attached to his jacket. This is the last time I will ever see his face. I stand there holding his ring feeling completely numb. I've been given his ring and now they are taking him away.

After his death, I tried to move forward and in some ways, I have. I've made life decisions without him. Our kids are on new journeys. Every single day I think of him. Not just once, but countless times. Sometimes I'm angry at the way he left us and how it has affected not only me, but our children. I'm left alone to hope it will not impact them negatively years from now. I'm sad he isn't experiencing life with us. Then, I wonder what kind of life we would be experiencing if he were still here, again with mixed emotions. I miss him every day. I miss our conversations. Not our shower sessions, but the conversations about everything and nothing. That was his forte. He could talk about anything and nothing with anyone and it was always interesting. I miss hearing his voice. Listening to the five voicemails I saved just doesn't cut it.

I still struggle to move forward every day. I have found through the process, that it is harder now than it was in the beginning. The first six months after he died I was doing well. I cried a lot, but I also laughed. I was free to live again. The one outlet I relied on was the gym my husband and I used to go to. At first it was comforting to be there. Before long it became the hardest place for me to be. There were so many memories of us there that it was hard to go and not think of him. I couldn't get past it. Being able to take care of myself became less of a priority. I began to focus all my attention on everyone else that needed to be taken care of.

I'm just now learning that I'm worth my time. This is not an easy phrase to remind yourself of everyday, but it is necessary. My focus now is on the life I want for myself and helping my kids achieve their goals. My children and I will not be seen as victims. The life we experienced with my husband was often tainted with fear, anxiety and self-protection, but it was also good. At first it was hard to separate the good memories from the bad. I'm learning how to do that. This is a process that is worth the work.

If this story is a reflection of your life, do not do what I did. Don't take it all on yourself. Don't let yourself become isolated and led to believe that you are the only one that understands them. This kind of belief can lead to your loved one feeling like you are not only the one they can tell everything to, but the one that they lash out at physically, emotionally and psychologically. He knew I would never give up on him. There were no longer boundaries in our relationship.

There has to be boundaries.

You have to remember your worth and your need to live. Saving and taking care of yourself is equally as important as helping your loved one. You have to realize and accept that you can't fix them. You can support them, but they need to find that desire to live within themselves. Push them to get help. Sometimes finding the right help takes time and effort, but that is easier to deal with than death. Never give up on someone you love. They are worth it.

If you are the one suffering with PTSD and any of this resonates with you, reach out. Reach out for help and never stop. Try to remember you are more than the time you spent overseas. The things you saw and/or did, are not the only things that make you who you are. You were someone before and you have a chance to begin again. Hold on to the good.

Sometimes I think of that q-tip. It still lies in the same spot it always has, in my jewelry box. I know now that it is not all I have left of my husband. I had a love that was passionate and extreme. A love that existed throughout all of this. A love that I never gave up on. I never doubted and still do not doubt that he loved all of us, his unit. I have four amazing children that we made together. I learned many things about myself and others while on this journey. I will cherish every good memory and look forward to remembering them without remembering the bad.

MY BROTHER'S KEEPER
Nathan "Thumper" Johnson

Nathan served as an infantryman with U.S. Marines and deployed twice with the 26th and 24th Marine Expeditionary Unit (Special Operations Capable). During his final deployment, he participated in OEF (Operation Enduring Freedom) and then as a ground element of Task Force Tarawa, during the initial invasion of OIF1 (Operation Iraqi Freedom). After his enlistment, he entered the private sector as an independent contractor. This story shows the relationship Nathan had with his brother, also a combat veteran, and the jaded views some might have towards an issue they might not fully understand until it's too late.

One of the last conversations I had with my brother was in regard to how he was handling the stress of his recent deployment. Matt was with the 502nd out of Fort Campbell, Kentucky, and his last deployment had him out for 11 months. He had missed all the major holidays, the birth of my son and the best man position at my wedding. He had a short leave block scheduled in the summer of 2006 and as always, we met up for drinks and some much-needed "bro time." We met up at our parents' home and spent the day out in the backyard, waist deep in the pool tossing a football, drinking beers and catching up. The previous Summer he and I met up for lunch out at Camp Victory. I was security contracting at the time and he was passing through BIAP (Baghdad International Airport) on his way back to his FOB (Forward Operating Base) in Muhammadiyah. We had a few laughs about the Toby Keith USO tour that we had both had the opportunity of missing due to being out on operations; Matt with his unit and me with my convoy security detail.

Matt and I were half-brothers; he was six years my junior. Over the past three years we had grown close after I had recommended he drop his dead-end factory job in Oklahoma and join the military. In 2004, Matt got his GED and enlisted in the Army as an 11-B (Infantryman). I was as proud of him as any brother could be.

"No big loss, would've rather seen the Dallas Cowboy Cheerleaders," we laughed.

Both of us had been deployed for Christmas of 2005 so we were looking forward to spending the upcoming holidays together with the family. I laughed and shrugged off the missed holiday. I told my brother how I had spent that Christmas up in Mosul at Camp Diamondback getting drunk and living in a Conex box that's only redeemable feature was a 24hr porn stream on my TV. Matt went quiet for a moment, looking down at his beer and setting the football at the edge of the pool.

"I spent Christmas day patrolling an area where we had been hit hard by an IED the day before," he said. "We lost a couple guys, a few cherries, some we didn't find but others we only found parts of. I found a boot on the side of the road with a foot still in it... belonged to a friend of mine. I saw his name on the dog tag."

He tilted his head and finished his beer.

"Fuck, brother. I'm sorry," I replied.

Matt cracked open another beer. "Fuck it," he said. "Fuck 'em, I wish I could kill them all. Every last one of them ragheads."

"You and Toby Keith?" I joked. "Maybe he'll write a song about it."

Matt shook it off. Shook off that far away stare one gets when reliving a painful memory and with my brother, I knew

64

there were many.

"Bro, if anything is ever bothering you, don't hesitate to call me," I told him. "You can't drink it all away and shit like that... you can't confide in a girlfriend unless you want to scare the hell out of her and make her think you're crazy. Believe me, I know. There's things I don't even speak with my wife about. We can talk shop amongst ourselves because we are the only ones who understand... everyone else will pat your head and give you a pill and diagnose you with PTSD."

"PTSD is a fucking joke," he shot back. "The only fuckers claiming that shit are fat-assed fobbits [people that don't leave the FOB] who've never left the wire or scamming pieces of shit too lazy to get a job after they ETS [expiration - term of service]."

I didn't disagree with him. I thought back to how many people I knew that had gone running to the VA with extravagant claims of how awful their lives had become post-military. The same guys who grow beards, wear their security contractor ball caps with a Punisher skull patch and strut into Applebee's for a free meal on Veterans Day with their "Pay-attention-to-me-because-I'm-a-Vet" t-shirt and post-service "Ooh-Rah" tattoos. The guys regaling civilians in a bar with their heroics one day, while crying to some VA shrink the next.

"Fuck 'em all, bro... fuck 'em all."

We spent the rest of the afternoon drinking beers and talking. I assured my brother that there was a whole world of opportunities waiting for him when his time with the Army came to an end. My plan was to get him into the contracting community where the rules were a little looser and the paycheck was a lot bigger. Matt confided in me that his next deployment would be his last. For a moment, I was confused. He explained.

"I watch these fuckers kill each other, try to kill us. We kill one and ten more just like him show up the next day. One day you're smoking and joking with your boys, the next day you're picking up pieces of them to send home to their mothers. Just a matter of time before someone's picking up pieces of me."

"I'm not coming home," he said. "Not this time."

I gave him what reassurance I could. Told him not to worry and that we all get the jitters sometimes. The strange thing was... for some reason I knew what he was saying was true. As we finished our conversation and the last of our beers, I pulled the tab off my can and put it on my keychain. I had an uneasy feeling that it may be the last drink I'd have with my brother. The next day I took my brother to the airport and hugged him tight before watching him make the lonely walk to his gate. I cried on the drive home.

Matt didn't make it to Christmas that year. He was stabbed while breaking up a bar fight off base while back home at Fort Campbell. A small, superficial injury that wasn't even life threatening. He sent a picture of his wound and laughed about his hangover being the worst part of it. I chastised him over it. He was going through a break up with his girlfriend, concerned about his upcoming deployment and drinking away the depression that was always glossed over in our conversations.

"Matt," I told him, "you can't save the world."

My brother went to the base hospital the next day and got a couple sutures and was prescribed a few painkillers. He sent me a picture and tried to call me, but I was working and unable to take the call. I had intended to call him back to chastise him a bit for his recklessness, but I never got the chance.

He went back to his room, took his meds with some vodka, went to sleep and never woke up.

My brother had post-traumatic stress disorder. He was never formally diagnosed and would have denied it if he was, seeing it as an admission of weakness. Matt's way of dealing with stress came from the comfort of a bottle and the occasional booze-soaked heart-to-heart with his big brother. The events leading up to his death, from childhood to his military service, were well beyond the stress limits of what the average person sees in their day-to-day lives. We knew this, Matt and I, but even if he were still with me, we would look at those claiming PTSD to be lesser men.

This doesn't mean that PTSD doesn't exist. It only means that we are too stubborn to acknowledge it while we see so many others exploiting it. To this day, I don't know if my brother committed suicide or if he was just careless. I've lost a handful of friends that I had served with and recently two co-workers to suicide. In each case I would not be surprised if PTSD was the common factor.

If you have a problem, seek help. If you need a brother to talk to, call me. If you're exploiting the system, you're an asshole.

CHALK TWO

This group consists of 3 members of the United States Marine Corps. They will show well-researched writing. They will show you the warrior ethos that molded them. They will show you what seeing their fellow Marines in pain does to a person. They will show you how a human being can be so lost and still find their way, so long as they keep pushing forward.

Two of these Marines knew each other very well as they deployed in the same unit together and the third has no idea who the other two are.

A SCARRED VETERAN OR AN EXPLOITABLE "GIFT"

Nelson Smith

Shell Shock... Battle Fatigue... Post-Traumatic Stress Disorder

Post-traumatic stress disorder PTS(D) is an evolved and complex condition derived from the aftermath of a traumatic event[s], which when left untreated or allowed to fester over a period of time can alter one's state of mind and produce PTS(D)-related symptoms. An individual diagnosed with PTS(D) can have a mild to severe impairment in any and all aspects of life, ranging from relationships to social and occupational functionality. In 1952, the American Psychiatric Association (APA) published its first edition of the Diagnostic Statistical Manual of Mental Disorders (DSM-I). It was not until 1980 the "APA added PTSD to DSM-III, which stemmed from research involving returning Vietnam War Veterans, Holocaust survivors, sexual trauma victims and others (Friedman, 2015)." Historically, PTS(D) has been linked to combat-related traumatic events; however, the DSM-III provided the "link between the trauma of war and post-military civilian life (Friedman, 2015). In 2013, the APA published its fifth edition (DSM-5), which serves as the current criteria for diagnosing present-day PTS(D). What I intend to share with the reader, particularly non-veterans, is a veteran's perceptive on PTS(D) before, during, and after combat based on my experiences and discussions with fellow veterans.

Before Combat:

Background: I joined the Marine Corps at the age of 19 and served from 2005 to 2009 as an Infantry Rifleman. Within those four years, I completed two combat deployments (2006 & 2007 – 2008) to Iraq with 1/1 Bravo Company. There was nothing fancy or high-speed about my short stint in the

Marines, so I will save the cool-guy stories for the next veteran. However, it was an experience like no other, from the fraternal brotherhood you become a part of to the continuous testing of one's mental and physical capabilities and limitations, and even experiencing the misery, death, and destruction that the war machine leaves behind. The good...the bad...and the ugly; I would not trade it for a thing, and if I had to do it all over again, I would. This is a common theme you will find among most veterans.

Like most growing up, I have heard the terms "shell shock" (WWI) and "battle fatigue" (WWII) used to describe the affects war has on the men who fought it. Anxiety, depression, home-sickness and nightmares or flashbacks are all common symptoms mentioned in history books or depicted in Hollywood films. Over time, books and films have introduced readers and viewers to things beyond the physical horrors of war, and immersed audiences in the psychological impact war has on the hearts and minds of those who've fought. Veterans of prior wars recount their experiences in documentaries, annual memorial ceremonies and between a grandfather and grandson to remind each generation, to quote former President Ronald Reagan, "Freedom is never more than one generation away from extinction. We didn't pass it to our children in the bloodstream. It must be fought for, protected, and handed on for them to do the same, or one day we will spend our sunset years telling our children and our children's children what it was once like in the United States where men were free." It is this fundamental principle that inspires individuals to voluntarily serve their country and answer a calling greater than themselves no matter the sacrifice or outcome.

The pre-combat phase or pre-deployment work-up is a top-down-bottom-up preparation and evaluation process of the unit as a whole. The U.S. military does an excellent job at replicating and immersing each deploying unit into the region of operation, from the cultural and environmental aspect to providing role players and conducting scenario-based exercises based on the latest enemy tactics, techniques and procedures (TTPs). The training closely simulates what one may encounter on the battle field in order to test the unit's overall capabilities, effectiveness and readiness. Each warrior is constantly reminded by his seniors that unnecessary casualties or deaths are due to one's failure to master the basics and consistently execute his duties and responsibilities. At the beginning of training, a warrior understands the stakes at hand (injury or death). By the end, his confidence is one of "invincibility" and his skills are honed to ensure it is the enemy who suffers, not himself or members of his squad.

During Combat:

Deploying to a combat zone is a young boot's (Marine) or cherry's (Army) final test to see what they are made of. All the hard work and long hours dedicated to the unit's pre-deployment training package are designed to prepare each warrior, platoon, company and the battalion for what lies ahead. All the blood, sweat, and tears (for some) have been paid and it is now time to collect. At the start of the deployment, the warrior is at his mental and physical peak in order to carry out the unit's mission and react and respond to any situation that may arise. His job, weapon drills, squad's standard operating procedures (SOPs) and contingency plans have been drilled into his head day-in and day-out in order to "locate, close-with and destroy the enemy, or repel the enemy's assault." Despite the variety of traumatic events that may take place and the loss of fellow warriors, whether injured or killed, the warrior simply does not have the luxury to mourn the fallen at that point in time. If someone was having a difficult time with a particular incident or loss, he is met with ample support from his peers and leadership. If it was beyond the squad leader or platoon sergeant's abilities, then a meeting with the Navy Chaplin or wizard (psychiatrist) can be arranged. The mission's high-tempo requires a mentally and physically healthy individual at all times, and a mental breakdown means one less man in the fight.

There are three essential elements that I believe shield, to an extent, a warrior from mentally breaking down during combat. First, is the consistent execution of one's duties and responsibilities within the squad (13 warriors). "You are only as strong as your weakest link," is a common phrase repeated throughout one's enlistment. A failure to maintain situational awareness, cover one's sector of fire, stay awake on post, etc. presents an opportunity for the enemy to exploit, which can result in a fellow warrior being wounded or killed. Knowing the life of the guy to your left and right is dependent upon you as you are dependent upon them is enough to mentally and physically stay strong and keep your head in the game. Second, is developing, strengthening, and nurturing the bond among the squad members. This bond can serve as a safeguard to mitigate mental fatigue and other stressors, as well as keep each other motivated because at the end of the day, no one is suffering alone in this fight. Lastly, the number one thing that affects troop morale is leadership. A leader who invests himself in his men, leads by example and earns the trust of his warriors can accomplish any mission and overcome any obstacle. I believe these three elements can waver in strength to a degree, but they synergistically keep the negative forces, including PTS(D), at bay.

After Combat:

PTS(D) does not discriminate; there are no set number of traumatic events before symptoms become noticeable or debilitating; it is not restricted by time; and no two diagnoses are the same. As more research and studies are conducted to better understand PTS(D) as a whole, previous findings and empirical data has brought the invisible wounds of war center-stage for much debate, discussions, and a call for action. According to the U.S. Department of Veterans Affairs (2015) National Center for PTSD, the "prevalence of PTSD in veterans:

- **Operations Iraqi Freedom (OIF) and Enduring Freedom (OEF)**: About 11-20 out of every 100 Veterans (or between 11-20%) who served in OIF or OEF have PTSD in a given year.

- **Gulf War (Desert Storm)**: About 12 out of every 100 Gulf War Veterans (or 12%) have PTSD in a given year.

- **Vietnam War**: About 15 out of every 100 Vietnam

Veterans (or 15%) were currently diagnosed with PTSD at the time of the most recent study in the late 1980s, the National Vietnam Veterans Readjustment Study (NVVRS). It is estimated that about 30 out of every 100 (or 30%) of Vietnam Veterans have had PTSD in their lifetime."

Despite these staggering numbers, PTS(D) is not a lifelong diagnosis. At least it does not have to be. PTS(D) is not limited to the traumatic events experienced in a combat zone, but includes adverse environmental and personal factors as well. Factors such as transitioning to post-military life; failed relationships and professional issues; self-medicating or excessive use of drugs and alcohol; or a combination thereof, can serve as stress multipliers and become a recipe for disaster. We all have a role to play to help our veterans. For the veteran, he or she has an obligation to his or her self, his or her family and to the fallen to seek early treatment to minimize and reverse the severity of his or her condition. One must peer into the mirror and come to terms with one's current mental, physical and spiritual state. Change must start with the veteran, but the journey does not have to be alone.

The private sector, charities and fellow veterans have answered the call by creating programs and services to serve as alternative treatments and support for wounded and struggling veterans. Treatment and assistance can range from utilizing social media platforms to connect with veterans or veteran social groups; becoming a member of your local veteran group like the Iraq and Afghanistan Veterans of America (IAVA), wilderness expeditions with Outward Bound, K-9 companionship with Southeastern Guide Dogs and Puppies Behind Bars, or enroll in a VA program.

Concerning the Veterans Affairs (VA), the VA is the poster child for what a single-payer government healthcare system looks like. For fiscal year 2017, the President's Budget Request is $182.3 billion for a department with roughly 341,000 employees whom service approximately 7 million out of 21 million veterans (VA, 2017). $182.3 billion for 7 million veterans and still veterans cannot receive the quality care, and in some cases, lifesaving care they need in a timely manner. The VA employs some wonderful people, but the department is drowning in scandals and rife with corruption, lack of transparency and accountability. I would advocate for a free-market approach for veteran's healthcare that will create competition amongst the private sector and VA hospitals and a federal assistances model that is similar to the Post-9/11 GI Bill in its flexibility and mobility, which empowers the veteran. Competition fuels innovation, improves the quality of products and services, lowers costs and provides timely service.

Not all combat veterans suffer from PTS(D), and not all veterans with PTS(D) are unstable or crazy. Do not pity those who do, but help those you can. Additionally, and it is infuriating, but there are a small percentage of veterans who have falsely claimed PTS(D) for financial gain and/or to use as a "trump-card" when conversing with civilians or fellow veterans. Karma is a bitch!

"Some people live an entire lifetime and wonder if they have ever made a difference in the world, but the Marines don't have that problem." - Ronald Reagan

References:
Friedman, M. (2015). History of PTSD in Veterans: Civil War to DSM-5. Retrieved from: http://www.ptsd.va.gov/public/PTSD-overview/basics/history-of-ptsd-vets.asp.

U.S. Department of Veterans Affairs (VA). (2015). PTSD: National Center for PTSD. How Common is PTSD? Retrieved from: http://www.ptsd.va.gov/public/PTSD-overview/basics/how-common-is-ptsd.asp.

U.S. Department of Veterans Affairs (VA). (2017). FY 2017 Budget Submission. *Office of Budget.* Retrieved from: https://www.va.gov/budget/products.asp.

THE SOUNDS OF FURY

Jake Jourdonnais

"INCOMING! EVERYONE STAY THE HELL INSIDE, STAY AWAY FROM THE WINDOWS, TAKE COVER, INCOMING!"

The whole sky started falling in on our heads as we dove for whatever cover we could find, either inside the half-finished brick house that made up our patrol base or outside, next to sandbags or concrete fixtures. We were hoping and praying that the next one wouldn't draw a bead on the cover we decided to take as our asylum. I sat there for a few seconds with the world spinning on its head as I choked on chalk-like dust and tried to gather my hearing after the blasts. Wearing only shorts, T-shirt and flip-flops, the ensuing chaos erupted into a battle charge to throw on flak vests, Kevlar helmets and boots, followed by grabbing rifles and radios. The squad leaders still inside were sending Marines up on the rooftop to plus-up the augmented positions (positions only manned in combat situations). As I awaited placement on the rooftop our Lieutenant came rushing through the doorway with blood on his helmet and face. All I remember was a Marine asking our Lieutenant if we had casualties outside and how many, to which our Lieutenant responded with, "Yes, it's a mess, everybody's hit."

Outpost (OP) Martini was a recently established patrol base on the outskirts of Al Karma and Subhayat, Iraq, in April 2006. Our OP was named after Lance Corporal Philip J Martini, a team leader in our squad who had been killed by a sniper just five days prior, while we were moving to support an additional Marine unit in heavy contact. Developed to launch squad size (13 Marines) mounted vehicle and foot patrols from, OP Martini was a show of force to the insurgency and a beacon of an increased security presence for the local people of Subhayat. It consisted of our platoon, a brick-made and dirt-floored abandoned house, and was surrounded by giant sand-filled

Hesco barriers. These barriers were neatly stacked side-by-side to form a square shaped, walled-off perimeter around the living quarters and fighting positions. Each Hesco was about the size of a utility shed and sat well above the height of an average man. Protection was offered from the four permanently manned over-watch positions, augmented positions and the manned ECP (entry control point). The ECP consisted of a maze of concrete jersey barriers just wide enough to let a vehicle or foot patrols through. OP Martini sat alone overlooking a desert wasteland to the north, contrasted by lush farm villages and the small town of Subhayat to the south. Recent Intel reports claimed the area was a hotbed of insurgent activity, to what extent wasn't clear, until the morning of April 13th.

Half of our platoon, or roughly fifteen Marines were outside conversing with the Company Commander's personal security detachment (PSD), consisting of thirty Marines and armored vehicles that had pulled in on a resupply mission right before the mortars hit. Their vehicles were sitting in a crescent moon shape in the center of the OP. The six to eight mortars that hit were very precisely "walked" in a line through the middle of the enclosed patrol base. Inside, the ear-splitting concussive blasts shook the walls, throwing debris through the open windows and doors. After hearing our Lieutenant's terse words and knowing the augmented rooftop positions were manned, it took only seconds to gather as much medical gear as we could carry and rush out the doorway. The scene unfolding before us would forever change me as I was a nineteen-year-old Private First Class just nine months into a four-year enlistment and two months into my first tour in Iraq.

Bodies were scattered in every direction. Some lifeless, some yelling in pain and some with horrific abdominal wounds. Some men had limbs barely attached, some called out my name or the names of other Marines to help them and some asked for their wives or loved ones. There were only two Navy Corpsman (medics) on scene to treat the twenty-plus casualties, one of which was wounded himself but continued to provide aid. This wasn't our first taste of stress under combat conditions, so we began aiding the Corpsman by starting with the first wounded Marine we came to and systematically moving from casualty to casualty. We then peeled off to help with stretchers to begin carrying the casualties to cover. One by one each casualty was treated and carried into the brick building, the patrol base living quarters that had become our CCP (casualty collection point). Helicopters began landing to evacuate the more serious casualties (Urgent Surgical). A mounted Humvee evacuation for the less seriously wounded (Urgent) was rounded up as well. After the casualties were loaded, I hauled myself up on the rooftop to aid in over-watch while the Humvee's rolled out and the last helicopter disappeared through a cloud of dust. I could feel the helicopter's rotor blades thumping inside my sweat and blood-soaked flak and Kevlar as they ascended into the hot desert air. Later, a team of us assembled to head back outside to gather the mountains of gear that had been left behind in the chaos. Among the multitude of things gathered, I remember leaning down and picking up a shrapnel peppered Kevlar helmet covered in blood. Inside, taped to the Kevlar, sat a picture of a Marine's loved one. Lance Corporal Perez was among the Marines that lost their lives that day.

The event lasted no more than two hours in its entirety. Three Marines were killed and over twenty Marines and Sailors wounded. Before we had time to digest what had just happened, a few hours later we were sent out on a routine security foot patrol into the city to resume our normal operations. From the many detained, we did not find the insurgents responsible, no matter the efforts put forth during raids or Intel gathering. Anger and frustration slowly build as one continues this routine. A day in the life of a Marine Infantryman at war.

I wish those were the only Marines and Sailors killed or wounded from our unit throughout my two tours in Iraq from 2006-2008. Unfortunately, they were not. I served one tour as a squad point man. The other as a team leader and squad leader in Saqlawiyah, Iraq between 2007 and 2008. In a position of leadership, you make split-second decisions that can result in your Marines being killed or injured. Secondary in my mind, though still important, are decisions you make that lead to civilians being killed in the act of doing the former.

My time in Iraq wasn't just filled with horrific memories. The majority of it was made up of exciting times, funny times and long droughts of sheer boredom. Occasionally, I got to do some cool-guy stuff and there were also times when it felt like we were making a difference for the better. That's not what I want to write about here though. Rather, I am writing about the invisible war that most combat veterans to one degree or another deal with in life, during or after service: Post-Traumatic Stress Disorder. It's important to take the time to talk about what comes after a combat veteran's service. This topic is important because it covers the side of war that isn't romantic or compelling and leaves a lot of us feeling exposed, weak, or uncomfortable. However, this topic needs far more attention than any other component of our experiences and seeking help should be seen as an act of courage.

The symptoms associated with PTSD are vast and varied. They can be anywhere from intrusive/unwanted memories, avoidance of the subject, hopelessness, changes in emotional reactions like irritability, aggressiveness or depression and even overwhelming shame or guilt. Many of the symptoms aren't visible at first, but later manifest into visible symptoms like alcohol and prescription drug dependency. Generally, you will not find us digging a chest deep fighting hole in the front yard while wearing dog tags as Hollywood would have you believe. I just shared a very real and personal experience with the reader not for attention or sympathy, but rather to have you understand some aspects on how much an experience like that changes you... only to come back home a short time later to people talking about their Facebook status, summer vacations and getting invited to functions where you're the center of attention when all you really want is to be left alone. You go from an environment that demands round the clock alertness for months to an environment that is safe, secure and comfortable. You might as well be on the moon. It may sound strange, but all you think about is coming home while you're deployed and yet deployment to a combat veteran in many respects is less terrifying than getting home and realizing how much has changed. You miss the safety net that a squad of your brothers provides. You have direction and a cohesive mission. You sweat and bleed together. Much of your thought process is taken care of for you. You're trained, both mentally and physically, to carry out missions to kill or capture the enemy. You're given the tools and adequate equipment (most times) to do just that. The Marine Corps did very well in shaping me to carry out these tasks in a war zone, as they should. The hard part was being re-released back into society without your brothers, without direction, without a social filter and a head full of problems you haven't quite worked out yet.

It's also important to note that I don't blame anyone or any organization for the decisions I have made in my life. They were mine and mine alone and I take full responsibility. It was my decision to sign a dotted line giving four years of service to a country at war. It was my decision to join the infantry. I wanted to go to Iraq. Though this is true, in regards to PTSD, combat veterans don't have much control over symptoms associated with their experiences. At least not right away. PTSD has a way of warping how you view situations in any given environment. Lines at a grocery store annoy the hell out of you for no apparent reason. Road rage is all in a day's work. Crowds brew anxiety. Loud noises startle. Imagine for a second you walk around a corner and your sibling or friend decides to scare you. Remember that jolt of adrenaline when it worked? Remember it subsiding quickly as you realized what just happened? That doesn't happen for a combat veteran recently returned from war. That jolt of adrenaline, when startled, leads to minutes of trying to calm yourself down and re-establish reality. That analogy pertains to fits of anger, anxiety, smells and sounds associated with flashbacks. Most combat veterans would tell you these emotions are felt to varying degrees and intensities based on each individual's experiences and their perceptions of those experiences. Some carry these issues with them for a long time, some for their entire life. These issues don't just affect the veteran; they have a negative effect on wives, kids and family members as well. It affects a veteran's ability to seek employment, leading to an ever-increasing homeless and jobless veteran community. For three Marines from our unit, it led to taking their own lives.

The last thing a veteran with PTSD wants is to be treated like they're a psychiatric invalid. We're everyday people who want to move on and become productive members of society. Living with PTSD often feels like a personal struggle, but it doesn't have to be. Many private charities, non-profits, organizations and groups have been constructed to help veterans and their families transition. These charity groups include **IAVA** (Iraq and Afghanistan Veterans of America), an organization currently serving 2.4 million veterans. Another is **Wounded Warriors Family Support**, an organization started by retired Marine Colonel John Folsom in 2003. **Home for Our Troops** is helping severely injured veterans to build mortgage-free and specially adapted houses for multiple amputees. The **DAV** (Disabled American Veterans) is the most long-lasting veteran's advocacy and assistance group in America, helping claim benefits for 300,000 veterans and their families in 2015 alone. As for the **VA** (Veterans Affairs), they have been plagued by backlogged services, departments that are meant to deal with the influx of veterans leaving the service, as well as the many veterans who have served before us. It's important to list them here because the VA is probably the most visible service to veterans. Some of their services have improved to include veteran PTSD help groups, but I believe they are behind in their provisions of treatment and care. The VA, in my experience and opinion, should be consulted secondary to the organizations listed above.

For myself, coming home and dealing with my experiences later healed themselves by many things. None of them though... were as important as time. I lost enjoyment with a lot of activities I loved before the service. In time, they came back to be as enjoyable as before, if not more so. Like any wound that needs healing, healing starts from the inside and it takes time... time dependent on the severity of the wound. Outside influences are important and necessary, but ultimately, it's on the individual to take the steps to heal. Knowing you're not alone is important. I was fortunate enough to have a very loving and caring family; they were instrumental in helping me while deployed and after I left the service. I met Lyndsey, a great girl whom I love very much. She has showed me the error of my ways many times. I started traveling and hunting again, learned how to rock climb and scuba dive. I started climbing mountains. I've kept in touch with Marines that I had served with, another massive healing aid, and attended some group meetings. I've found a way to emulate combat's adrenaline rush and camaraderie with healthy, challenging, lifelong experiences.

Sometimes, life just doesn't feel like life if you're not on the edge of it every once in a while. I believe our brothers who gave their lives in the service of their country would want us to live in such a manner that would honor that sacrifice.

I will always be proud that I served in a combat unit during a time of war with some of the best men I've ever known. The only blessing in combat is witnessing some of the greatest acts of bravery and selflessness under some of the most extreme environments.

My goal and the subsequent information here were meant to shed some light on the effects of PTSD during and after combat, as well as the help available and the ways in which I found asylum. I have, by no means, suffered from the worst of PTSD symptoms, compared to many who served or are currently serving. My only hope is for all veterans to find a little peace from any troubling experiences. Never question the honor and fortitude it took in choosing to serve. Stand behind that decision like a rock and never sway from it, no matter how troubled you may feel. Seek out your own asylum, one that promotes success and longevity. Always keep family, friends and brothers-in-arms close.

In the words of war journalist Sebastian Junger...

"War is life multiplied by some number no one has ever heard of."

I say live life as a veteran in that same multiplied manner.

Black Horse: Honoring My Ancestors in War

Phillip Chavez

"Live your life that the fear of death can never enter your heart.
Trouble no one about his religion.
Respect others in their views and demand that they respect yours.
Love your life, perfect your life, beautify all things in your life.
Seek to make your life long and of service to your people.
Prepare a noble death song for the day when you go over the
great divide.
Always give a word or sign of salute when meeting or passing a
friend,
or even a stranger, if in a lonely place.
Show respect to all people, but grovel to none.
When you rise in the morning, give thanks for the light,
for your life, for your strength.
Give thanks for your food and for the joy of living.
If you see no reason to give thanks, the fault lies in yourself.
Abuse no one and no thing, for abuse turns the wise ones to fools
and robs the spirit of its vision.
When your time comes to die,
be not like those whose hearts are filled with fear of death,
so that when their time comes they weep and pray for a little
more time
to live their lives over again in a different way.
Sing your death song, and die like a hero going home."

~ Tecumseh

When we awake each morning, we should give thanks for life and think about how our lives have purpose for those around us; for the friends, family and the strangers we say hello to, or the helping hand we give to those who need an extra pair of hands or a kind word. Through my life, I have struggled with

85

many things like anger and sadness, but the thing that has stood true for me is the pursuit of purpose. In the Marine Corps, I found purpose with being part of a society of warriors; this elite group of men and women who find a purpose together in the love of comradery and strength. We created a bond that will forever be remembered and held true. And through this understanding I found my purpose as a father, husband, brother, friend and son. Each day I remember those friends I lost in war and remind myself that my life is no longer my own because I carry a part of them with me. With the stories I tell my kids or the local guys at the VFW, they live through me. My purpose is to honor their memory through living a good life and being the best man I possibly can be by making choices with honor, courage and commitment to the values we as warriors hold high and true.

I grew up in Colorado where my grandfather taught me to hunt and fish. Through these teachings, I have learned many things about nature and the natural order of things. Through the indigenous teachings from family and friends, I have learned to listen to those feelings that nature communicates with us and embrace the connection we have with every living thing. My indigenous culture has helped me overcome many things when I returned from war. I found understanding in our ceremonies and healing. I feel grateful that our indigenous culture knew war and understood that life was a balance and with the power of prayer and ceremony we can find peace and purpose.

I fought in OIF II (Operation Iraqi Freedom II). I served with 1st Battalion 4th Marines, Bravo Company, Weapons Platoon as an infantry machine gunner. We floated over with the 11th MEU (Marine Expeditionary Unit) in 2004 to Kuwait where we climatized to the harsh desert life for some time and then pushed into Najaf, Iraq. When we first arrived in Najaf, we quickly fell into the rhythm of the war machine; standing long post and long patrols not knowing what to expect. Things quickly escalated when one of our CAAT teams (Combined Anti Armor Team) got ambushed and we got called out for QRF (Quick Reaction Force). We were baptized by fire that day and set a tone. The next day we were called out on QRF to set a defense around a downed helicopter so it could be loaded and secured. As we set our defense with tracks and dismounts, we set a VCP (Vehicle Control Point) but things quickly got hairy when we started to take small arms fire from the cemetery across the street. As we took fire, a car refused to stop and in fear of a VBIED (Vehicle Borne Improvised Explosive Device) we opened fire. As the car slowed to a stop filled with bullet holes and blood splatter on the windows, the marines at the VCP slowly approached the vehicle. As they opened the back door they found an older woman still alive and just like that, the Docs went to work trying to stop the bleeding. One of my buddies ran over to get the gurney to carry the women to the nearest HUMVEE that would take her to the hospital. As they carried the body away, I remember thinking...

"Is this real? Did this just happen?"

As they finished loading the helicopter, we moved back to the FOB (Forward Operating Base). When we pulled into our area, the air seemed different. The look on everyone's faces was like a trance, because the day before we took fire and returned fire, but the truth of combat came to life in the sight of death. As we stood joking, trying to make light of what just happened, I felt weird like I was there... but not. A few days went by and we would take random small arms and mortar fire every day until the day we lived in constant war. We were a track company, so when we got the green light to hit the cemetery, we started constant remedial training on how to unload from a track and set lines to push forward and lots of contact drills. We practiced and practiced till everything was more muscle memory than actual thinking. Before loading up we had a little time to just hang out, prepare mentally and, for me, prepare spiritually with my native buddies. We smudged down and prayed with tobacco for bravery, and if death came for us, we would not have fear. We told jokes and gave thanks that we few men were going to follow the footsteps of our ancestors as warriors and go into battle like the stories we read as children. We joked about the stories we idolized as young men training for war. The word was given and we loaded up, with the anxiousness of young men about to play in the championship game, pumped each other up and took our positions. I remember loading up in the track with my 240Gulf and my M16 slung over my shoulder on air watch as we left the FOB. It was late afternoon when we left, and I will never forget the feeling and sounds that came next. As we got closer to the cemetery, we could hear small arms fire and the faint pinging on the tracks hull. We were locked and loaded as we hit the wall of the cemetery. It seemed like all hell broke loose and the back gate of the track dropped. Everyone rushed out except for myself and my buddy Castellon, who got stuck with track security with me. I was on top of the track laying some cover fire for the marines below as they pushed to cover. The dusk was lit up with green and red tracers as RPGs and mortars screamed all around. While I was firing, I turned to see an RPG flying in our direction. I watched in disbelief as the rocket flew over my head and I could feel the heat of it as it impacted on a wall next to the track. I slid down into the track with this crazy feeling of *holy shit, that just happened* and gave a chuckle as I told myself that was too close. I got back on top of the track and continued to fight. I don't remember how long it went on, but the fire slowed to almost nothing, the guys came back to load up in the tracks, we pulled out and returned to the FOB. We returned to the FOB with the true feeling of living through hell. Sure, we took small arms fire and mortar rounds before, but nothing to the ultimate chaotic, hellish fire fight we just experienced. I remember joking with my buddy Flores about how I almost shit my pants when one of our sergeants told us to knock it off because there were a few guys who literally shit their pants from being in the fire fight. I felt like the only way to deal with the craziness of what had just happened was to make light and joke about it. Otherwise, fear would have set in and I would not have been of any use to my brothers in a future fire fight. Maybe that's why we few have such a sick sense of humor that I feel will never leave me.

We continued to fight in the cemetery day in and day out for what seemed like months, but the day I will never forget is the day we lost Sgt. Harvey Parkerson. On August 18, 2004, we set in a defense on the north end of the cemetery. We pushed in about 80 yards when we took 120mm mortar rounds on our position. We took cover and I was on the far-left side of the defense when the word got to us that Myriks got hit and was being MEDEVACED out. It was soon after that we got hit again and after being hit the second time, they told us that Sgt. Parkerson was hit. It didn't look good, but he was being MEDEVACED back to the FOB. We soon loaded back up and headed back to the FOB. We rode in silence, not knowing if Sgt. Parkerson was alive or dead. When we got back, the huge weight hit us all when we learned that he didn't make it. I remember thinking, *no way he could be gone*, and then the memories started to pour into my head as I sat there in disbelief. I remembered when we were loading our sea bags and packs onto the USS Denver in San Diego and I had helped Sgt. Parkerson carry his sea bag onto the ship because he had his wife and children with him. He was saying good bye. And now he was gone. As I thought of his family, I grew mad because here I was at 20 years old with no family of my own. I hated that he was taken and not me because he had more to live for at the time. Then one more blow was unintendedly given when our gunny handed my buddy and I Sgt. Parkerson's gear from when he was hit. He asked us to clean it and as I turned in disbelief of what I was looking at, one of our corporals came up who was good friends with Sgt. Parkerson and took the gear from us. He told us he would do it. I remember feeling mad and sad but thankful and disappointed all at the same time. I wanted to carry my weight when asked to do something but wondered if it was for the best that I didn't. I carried that burden of guilt for years and years and learned that they called it survivors remorse. Every once in a while, I feel that guilt, but now I look at my children and wife and realize that I was needed in the future. I lost over twelve friends fighting in Iraq. A lot of them were friends from School of Infantry, SOI. But none hit home like the death of Sgt. Parkerson, who I respected and learned from. He showed and gave a boot ass lance corporal like me a little dignity and respect as a man.

The war continued with the great loss of a friend in our platoon, but the fight got a little more personal. After fighting in Najaf and Kufa we got orders to move north to Abu Ghraib Prison to support the 9th Military Police Unit and Operation Phantom Fury in Falluja. There, we quickly fell into urban combat, which was a little different than fighting in a massive cemetery. We had little support from the local community because of the amount of mortar and small arms defilade fire we took from the city every day and night. So, we took aggressive action in our patrols and it payed off. The local leaders came to use and said that if we stopped the knock and talks or door to door sweeps and aggressive patrols in the city, they would stop the attacks on the prison. And it worked because from that time on, we had little attacks in the area.

After spending a little more time in Abu Ghraib and doing patrols in Falluja, they moved us to FOB Lima outside Hit where we continued patrols. There, we finished our 9-month tour, which was supposed to be a 6-month tour. I remember packing my things and wondering what it was going to be like coming back to the world after experiencing all the things we did. The thought of freedom to go to the movies or eat at a restaurant was such a foreign feeling. Here we were never alone. The bonds between brothers was so strong and now things were going to change drastically.

We loaded up on the commercial plane and off we went back to a world that seemed like a foreign place. It took a lot to adjust, in a way, to life state side, and I don't think we ever fully adjusted. Part of me is still in Iraq wandering the ancient streets and hearing the call to prayer every morning. Being there, I learned the beauty of the Iraqi culture and the rich and old history that it has. I think in many ways I never hated the people I was fighting because the native teachings I had taught me that I fought and killed to survive; not in hate, but to live... to live for my family and those that have touched my heart in a way that can never be repaid. I have learned from talking with Vietnam vets and WWII vets that telling my stories would ease the pain and so far, it has. I know that I may have good days and bad days dealing with what I have experienced with life and death. But the knowledge of life I gained in war can never be measured and the brothers I have gained can never be taken lightly. My memories and stories will keep those I have lost and those who are still here alive forever, and by living an honorable life, it will only help to strengthen how we are remembered. The greatest honor was to serve with giants among men and to pass on to my children the stories of my brothers I served with. I would like to thank my brothers from 1/4 Bravo Company who saved my ass more times than I can count and to the toughest machine gun section 1/4 has seen. We will forever be remembered in history.

This concludes Chalk Two

RESUPPLY 2

A Marine and a SEAL Team member.

A Lone Bastard

Kevin "Mac" McEnneny

Mac served in the Marines during "Don't ask, don't tell."
He happens to be gay.

"...and the rockets' red glare, bombs bursting in air, gave proof
through the night that our flag was still there..."

I was eighteen, my hand over my heart standing on the edge of a high school pool before our meet. My brother was deployed to Iraq and I thought to myself during this prelude, "Is this what he is going through right now? What's going to happen when he gets back? What if he has PTSD? What the hell is PTSD really, and is it as bad as people say?" I had just signed up for the Marines myself. What's going to happen when I go over there? Well, over the next six years I will get my answers. The unit I would soon join was in Iraq at the same time as my brother. They were suffering the worst casualties in modern U.S. and Marine history.

I joined the United State Marine Corps Reserves at the age of 17 and I was beyond excited, but also nervous as hell. You might be thinking "Yes, you should be nervous. You're joining the biggest and baddest fighting force in the world during a time of war." That didn't faze me. I knew I was going to join the Marines from a very young age and, at the time, I thought I was mentally prepared for that. However, one thing I didn't think about was the fact that I was gay. I joined in 2007 when don't ask, don't tell was alive and kicking. President Bush was still in office and it was a time in this country when myself and fellow homos did not see any changes to this policy coming anytime soon. I was out to a few friends in middle school and completely out in high school. Out of pure fear of slipping up and having to go back in the closest, I decided I would join the reserves. It would be easier for me to hide there. My recruiter was not too happy on this fact. He kept telling me that he sees something in me and that I would do great things in the fleet. He kept asking me to go active and told me I wouldn't regret it. I really wanted to go active, but my fear of getting kicked out added weight to this decision. As a senior in high school, I thought, "I can do one year in the fleet and possibly get kicked out or six years in the reserves and possibly do more good." It was always awkward when he kept asking why I was so hell-bent on joining the reserves. Like some little weasel, I made something up.

Bootcamp came and passed. Outside of all the mind games the drill instructors liked to play, they made sure to drill something into our heads...

"Everyone in this squad bay will be deploying. It doesn't matter if you're active or reserves and at least three people in this room will not make it home."

This was interesting for me because my brother was in Iraq the entire time I was in boot camp. It was also laying the ground work on how I thought to combat PTSD. Post-traumatic stress disorder; I took that literally as don't get stressed. It's that simple, right? Prepare yourself now, go over and over in your head any and every situation that you can think of. Realize that those scenarios can become reality. At my MOS (military occupational specialty) school I picked up the knowledge like a sponge in water. My MOS was 0621 Field Radio Operator. I was at the top of my class for knowledge and almost overall. My scrawny ass could run 3 miles in 20 minutes but couldn't get over 12 pull ups. My knowledge of radio and the operations of a COC (Command Operations Center) would later put me into the spot I was in when deployed to Afghanistan.

One thing about being in the reserves is that you're a part of the local community before even joining. Before joining and while in the DEP (delayed entry program), I volunteered at the local USO (United Service Organizations). I brought food for the marines who were at my future unit just to do something, anything for them. I helped fundraise for care packages for service members deployed. Little did I know that I was seeing the effects of PTSD in all these groups. While volunteering at the USO, I would talk to veterans from Vietnam who were also volunteering or working for the USO. These great men would tell me stories and give me some advice. One went a little more in depth about his war experiences. I listened to him talk about it so vividly after 30 plus years. I didn't even think twice about his life in the years that had passed since he saw combat. This army veteran told me how he was combat promoted to captain from E-7 because they had no officers. They kept getting killed. I just thought at the time, "Well, yeah that happened. I saw it in the movies." I couldn't comprehend the real meaning behind his words nor how much it had to take out of him for telling his story.

I also volunteered for a group called MOM: Mothers of Military. For the most part, I didn't really mind going to these groups. Sometimes I had to be persuaded. I still went, but it took a while to realize why they wanted me there. These mothers would get together, laugh, cry and sometimes show physical effects of the stress they were going through, especially when the local reserve unit was going through hell. I saw the love they had for their sons and daughters who were deployed. I met mothers whose sons just got to the fleet and got a tattoo, then a car. I got to be around these mothers and saw what was in their future. They just wanted a son there.

Communications school was over and it was time for me to check into my unit. My brother was home on his post deployment leave and gave me a once over after I squeezed into my pickle suit. The reserve unit was under renovations and I was wandering around to find the admin trailer. I walked in wide-eyed, confused, hoping I was in the right place and on time. I'm greeted by a senior chief who played into my insecurities and yells, "You checking in, boot?" Quickly looking at his collar I see the anchor and say, "Yes, chief." Great, I already fucked up. "Excuse me?" he responded (in the marines we call everyone by their exact rank). I looked again, seeing the star above his anchor and replied, "Excuse me. Senior Chief." After a good few minutes of normal "fuck, fuck games" with a new boot checking in, the situation got serious.

"Do you know what has happened to this unit?" the Senior

Chief asked.

"Yes," I responded.

"Good. Don't even think about talking to any of them."

Two or three months passed and it was the second drill since all hands-on deck. Like I've mentioned before, I went to high school in the same city that my unit was in. I knew a sister of one of the corporals in my platoon. We did not know each other well even though she and I had some of the same classes and were a part of the same extracurricular groups. However, we were connected in the sense that both our brothers were deployed to Iraq at the same time, even though they were in different branches of the military. After some concert or meet, her family hosted the after party. I went to the kitchen to get a drink and saw a USMC magnet on the kitchen door. Her mother was in the kitchen and I mentioned that I just joined the Marine Corps. She mentioned that her son was a part of the reserve unit that was deployed and I told her that's the unit I just joined. When she told me this, I could see the same pain in her eyes that I saw in my own mother's eyes. This is a real cost of war. It's not just about the men and women deployed, but the suffering the families go through as well.

As a young private first class and only at my second or third drill, with the word of that Senior Chief echoing in my head, I decided to go find this corporal and introduce myself. Well, that was a huge mistake. I believe it was these guys' first drill since coming back from Iraq after losing 49 brothers in 6 months. Our unit had an atmosphere that anyone that wasn't a part of the 2005 deployment just didn't talk to the marines that just got back. The wounds were too fresh. These marines were beaten and you could read it in their faces, but it was covered by anger and sorrow. As a boot, you best not even talk to them. I found the corporal I was looking for talking with another corporal that just got back. I started to walk up to them thinking this was simply the older brother of a friend of mine. The second I went up there, the other marine looked at me and screamed in my face.

"What the fuck are you thinking that you have the right even approach us?"

98

"Is your sister, x and mom, x," I stumbled over my words to the older brother corporal.

"Yeah, how the fuck do you know that?" he asked.

"I went to high school with your sister."

Without skipping a beat, the other marine chimed in...

"Oh dude, he fucked your sister."

Normal talk for marines, but with my mind racing and playing so many situations in my head, this might be a normal situation to most marines, but not for me. One, I had never been accused of having sex with a woman before... gross. As a civilian, I could usually shut it down with a quick response like, "Yeah, my faggot ass really fucked your sister." But as my mind raced, I couldn't say that here. I was lost. So, I went quiet. Well, that didn't help my situation. Silence admits fault, right? This little deal and normal banter between marines took me through a tremendous loop. When I was trying to hide being gay, I would say, "Yeah, I totally railed her," but this was his sister and a supervisor of mine. What do I do in this situation? Well, they quickly said, "Get the fuck out of here and you ask permission to talk to us again." These are completely normal games to play on boots and I did the same thing as time passed, but always in the back of my mind I was so worried about these people finding out my little secret. That would be it for me. That situation made me realize I must come up with a back story with as few holes as possible. It even caused me to call my best friend growing up and ask him how to be with a girl. Like what's an appropriate number of fingers. It was a hilarious conversation, but one I never thought I would need to have.

Eventually, one of the marines that deployed in 2005 took me and a few other marines under his wing because he saw "great potential in us." He was the go-to person for all radio questions and the little nerd in me was very excited to learn even more. Outside of drills, we became very good friends. Jack got a good contracting job for a government agency in Huntsville. After one drill I was off work for the next few days and said I would drive down with him. We stayed in Cleveland that Sunday night at one of his friend's houses. We went to a local bar and Jack started to open up about his deployment. It was very eye opening. He told me the story about how he got his purple heart. He would go into detail about the surroundings, sights, smells and how he didn't realize he was hurt right away. When he told me his memory, it was like he wasn't drinking the beer next to me. His point of focus was somewhere else. His eyes couldn't look directly into mine and the tone of his voice was somber. As someone in the military, especially one who has all their siblings in at the same time, you learn how to read people and their story. Jack's story wasn't like the Chili's waiter who failed out of boot camp and tries to lie about it, only talking about boot camp and says he was stationed at Pendleton, but gives a Lejeune unit address. When Jack went into the details it was like he was telling me this while he was still in Iraq. How the story was told, the details remembered, the somber voice and the look on his face reminded me of a few other stories I heard; the Vietnam Captain at the USO or even stories my grandfather has shared with me. Now at that point in my life I had never heard a bad story about WW2, but that would all change after I went to war myself. I then saw the real effects of war. It wasn't just an older war veteran, but a good friend of mine. Looking back now, I still didn't really understand what he was saying. I knew what it was and saw the harsh realities of it, but I didn't really, truly understand it.

I am the type of person that strives to be the best at my job. I want to know everything. While in the marines I made sure I knew everything I could about all our radios and operations. Our unit was slated for a deployment to Afghanistan. During our work up, before we deployed, we had a third party come in to train us on how the new COC would be operating. This specific training was over two weeks and had multiple radio operators working the same role. After the training was completed, we had a debrief with everyone involved in the training. This included all the higher ups, including our battalion commanding officer, sergeant major, gunner, all the way down to the private. During the debrief, the contractors called me saying that of all the times they have done this training, all over the country, they never had this young and inexperienced radio operator handle the position so well in this simulation. They even tried to bombard me with multiple things at once that would never really happen and I handled it. This was a double edge sword for me. I was then on the radar of my most senior officers and staff noncommissioned officers, but also called out in front of my peers. It's not like I didn't put in the work.

I did have something to prove, not only to myself, but if it ever came down to it and if I was ever outed, I wanted to be the best so maybe they would look the other way.

When it came to rank, I was the type of person that would respect rank, but never cared if I personally got promoted. I had a habit of voicing my opinion in good stride. If someone said something I knew wasn't true, I would correct them regardless of rank. I thought I would do it respectfully, but this wouldn't make some people very happy. I had a personal motto that this isn't a meeting for a new burger launch. If you don't have the right information or know how to properly do something, it can be life or death especially with communications in a grunt unit. If our guys don't have proper communication setup or an operator that didn't know their job, how are we going to preform when they got in the middle of a firefight?

We went to Camp Pendleton for our official work up and there were rumors that we were going to have a TACP (Tactical Air Communication Party) team just in case our mission changed. This is something I always wanted to be a part of. TACP is a special team that is on the ground on front lines that call in the artillery, air and ship fire. Who wouldn't want to be a part of this? It's usually only E-5 and above, FACs (Forward Air Controllers - these are only officer pilots) or JTACs (Joint Tactical Air Controller - only enlisted, but the same job). These officer pilots or E-7 and above go through a special school to be able to clear these groups for fire. To be a part of this group you can only be one of three MOS's. Of course, I wasn't going to be a JTAC but they can have their own radio operators attached to them. I bombarded my gunny to be able to do at least one training with our Battalion FAC. For the first training, he was going to send our platoon sergeant and told me if he doesn't want to do it, he would send me. After the first training, I talked to our platoon sergeant and he let me take over. Now I was our FAC's radio operator. It was an awesome experience.

During our entire workup, if there was any training with the FAC, I got to be a part of it. Our FAC was a captain and an attack helicopter pilot. We got along very well and had a great mutual respect for each other. Anytime he had radio questions, he would run it through me, even if someone else gave him an answer. The pretty much made me his right-hand man. A group called ANGLICO (Air Naval Gunfire Liaison Company - a group that is pretty much the special forces of TACP) was at Pendleton at the same time as our workup and had a British counterpart training with them. We did live fire exercises with fixed wing (fighter jets), a few runs with rotary wing (attack helicopters) and the Brits had their own motormen. To this day, working with ANGLICO and the Brits doing live fire exercises using top of the line gear and dropping 500lbs bombs, being the youngest and least ranked marine or sailor there, was one of the highlights of my marine career. Our battalion mission was slated for SECFOR (security force) and off we went to Camp Leatherneck in Afghanistan. If the mission did not change, our battalion would not need a TACP team. Our mission didn't change and I was relocated to a job that had nothing to do with radio communications, but it would be a part of a rotating post watch for the largest marine base in Afghanistan. I was pretty pissed about this. I worked so hard to be one of the best in my field. I would get calls during our work up from my peers that were at a company or platoon level daily on how to work or set up a radio system. I could walk them through all menus and steps even without a radio in front of me. Now, I'm going to spend 12 hours a day looking at the desert. Well, the second day of being in country, that changed.

We got in country and someone knocked on the door of the "can." Can is slang for our little metal hut that housed eight to twelve marines. It was an H&S Company first-sergeant saying, "Mac, come with me." We walked down to a different can and there was a lieutenant, gunny and a staff-sergeant. The first-sergeant told me that I was being reassigned to 3rd platoon, Lima Company as their platoon radio operator. There was a situation with the current radio operator and the gunny of that platoon, so we were getting swapped out. The next day I fell into their formation. This was a little weird for me. I've always been at the battalion level. Yes, I have worked with grunts many times before, but never as a peer like this. I never fell into their formations nor had I been attached to them like this. I just taught classes on basic radio operations or I was part of a team that worked alongside them. About a week in country, we were doing on-call trap missions. Then, we got word that we will be going to Marjah and will be attached to 2/6. You hear all the time that you have to train like you'll be on the front lines, because you never know what will change and I was living proof of this. I was at the battalion level the entire time during our workup. I was passed over for extra training for MOUT or anything combat related because I was always going to be at the battalion level command operations center, then got pushed down to SECFOR and now I'm at a platoon level getting sent to the front lines after a week in country.

There truly are no closer brothers than an infantry brotherhood. I could see that from day one of being attached to this platoon. After just meeting these guys for the first time as we pack up to ship off to one of the most dangerous cities in Afghanistan, I can only imagine what's going to happen with my "correcting people" attitude, frame of mind and not being a grunt. Attached to these guys, we were about to see the true face of war. I knew I would have to gain their trust, but how? Night has fallen and we load up in a bird to fly over to our new home for six months. Troop transfers were only done during night cover because the area was too dangerous for day travel. We landed at FOB (Forward Operating Base) Marjah and were greeted by the 2/6 battalion commander and sergeant-major. We all funnel into a meeting room where they officially greet us and have a mini brief on what we will be doing. They opened for questions and, of course, with that high of a rank speaking to us, no one really asked anything. Except me, because why not, right? I asked, "I know we will be getting briefed by the unit we are replacing, but I would like to ask what type of IEDs and fire have you seen in this area? Is it more PPIED (Pressure Plate), trip wire, or DFC (Direct Force Charge)? More SAF (small arms fire) than IEDs? Is it only SAF or are they using rockets as well?" As a new E-3 radio operator to this platoon, asking this type of question was a little abnormal. I wanted to show, as the new non-grunt, that I am taking this seriously and it was a way for me to show it. After the briefing I was approached by a few marines and a squad leader that said those were good questions. I felt that it was a stepping stone to prove myself worthy, that I took this serious and cared for our well-being. After two days at FOB Marjah we took a mounted patrol to our patrol base.

When we got to our new home, it was barely a patrol base. It was more like an outpost. It was in the shape of a triangle, had one long angled dirt wall and one with high Hesco bins for the back and side walls. There was also one layer of razor wire (type of barbed wire) surrounding the entire "base." The night we get to our new home, the current unit had a raid planned for a building called the bell tower. We had three squads in our platoon, but also had scout snipers attached to us. They immediately went to work and provided cover for the 2/6 unit that was doing this raid. The raid did not go very well and we lost a 2/6 marine the very first night we arrived by a DFC IED in the building. This was an eye opener for the six months to come.

The next morning I was getting briefed by the radio operator that was attached to that unit. They had a decent set up, but it was set up as an outpost rather than a patrol base, like what I thought we were going to be walking into. They had the metal quarter size quadcon that had the controls for the GBOSS (Ground Based Operational Surveillance System), a camera system that was 80 feet in the air that gave us a 360-degree view of our area. They had two radios set up with only one large OE-254 antenna that was on top of the quadcon for the company radio and a small radio attached "whip" antenna for the platoon radio. A little less than ideal set up, but expected for an outpost and for a unit that took over from the invasion force of Marjah. Nothing was built up yet. They slept under the stars on cots, in vehicles, or a few two man tents that were set up. We had about a week overlap with the unit we were replacing and it came from higher that we were going to turn this outpost into a fully functioning patrol base. During the transition period, we had combat engineers building up the base adding more Hesco bins and another row of razor wire. Of course, anytime you have combat engineers building a base, you're going to get shot at. Almost every day during the renovation, we either got pop shots or a short three-minute period of light fire.

Our mission when we took over was to continue to protect this stretch of road that was a heavily used log-train route. In the middle of our two patrol bases we were taking over, there was an S-curve in the road that was a high target for the enemy to lay IEDs to stop our trucks, supplies and troop movement. After the guys we replaced left, I knew I had to set up an ideal command center. I took this as my personal project and I was up for two nights, making the proper charts to track troop movement, detainees, up-to-date maps, color coded pins to log the location of any type of IED blast, SAF, mortar hits, firefights and any other related trackable instances. It was instilled in me when at the battalion level that a properly organized and operated command center will only give the best support when shit really hits the fan. I was also still trying to earn the trust and comradery of my grunt peers.

I kept up-to-date charts of the times, location and types of firefights and IEDs that were found. Before any patrol, I would brief the squad leaders on past incidents. I would inform them, "Just to let you know for this patrol scheduled today, we took SAF from this building at this time the last 2 weeks on this day. It's on your route, so keep your eyes open." For some reason, my lieutenant did not want me to go on foot patrols. He would openly say my job is too valuable and cannot be risked. Towards the end of my deployment I would find out the real reason he did not want me to go on patrols. This was a killer for me. I'm a platoon level radio operator. I'm supposed to be the one on the patrols with the radio, the most basic part of our job. Not only did this drive me mad, but it gave high resentment to my peers that had to carry the radio during these patrols and to hear the only reason they are is because my life is more valuable? It was complete bull shit. In the history of war, one of the highest targets is the radio operator. Take out the communications, take out their ability to call for reinforcements, air, medevacs, anything. It was just a part of my job and I wasn't allowed to do it.

For mounted patrols, I was a gunner. We had 32 marines and sailors in our platoon that were split up into two patrol bases. Less than half of us were below an NCO rank (E-3 or below). We were so undermanned and top heavy. When we went on mounted patrols, we left three marines at our patrol base. Thank god, the enemy never realized that. There were times we went out on a mounted patrol for 16 plus hours and it was a miracle that our base was never attacked. On large foot operations, I did go out. We had a week-long clearing operation where we slept in wadis, or abandoned buildings in the middle of "IED country" as we called it. We had extraction missions for HVT (High Value Targets) in our area of operation that Army special forces oversaw. They flew in at night and we provided their security for these missions.

One day I finally got to lay my head down for a few hours. It was a miracle if you got more than two hours of sleep in a 24-hour period. When I was asleep, we had two squads out on a foot patrol. I really tried to be on the GBOSS/radios every time a foot patrol went out, but we had an SNCO on the radios and thought it would be fine. I woke up to closer than normal gun fire. It's kind of crazy how you can hear it in your sleep and can tell the difference between whether if it's important or too far to be our problem. I jerk up and walk the 50 feet to our little makeshift COC and hear on the radio that it's our squads. This SNCO that was on watch for the radios, wasn't really. He's on the sat phone with a cigar in his mouth, trying to man the radios all at once. My anger was raised higher in that moment than any other time. He had no idea what he was doing and I had no idea what he was trying to do.

I took over the radios, got their grid (location) and plotted. I was about to report it up to the company level. However, on the company level was the platoon just north of us. They were the closest patrol base to us and they have a squad that's out and in a firefight at the same time. Over the company TAC, I get the grid from their firefight. After plotting it and realizing it looks more in-depth than a normal firefight, I get on the company TAC once it opens from the other squad and report our guys. They were split up into two teams, taking fire from an L shape formation while the other platoon's squad was in one group taking fire. After plotting all the grids with the two squads in three teams, I noticed that all friendlies were almost in a straight line with each other and the enemy was in a large area U shape. I think the company saw it as soon as I did because I requested a QRF (quick reaction force) and they said QRF was already in route. The QRF was coming out of the company location which was far from us.

By the time QRF got to us, the firefight was already broken up, but since they were already in route and close, they still decided to come to our patrol base anyway, just in case it pops off again. On this particular QRF was the battalion commander, battalion sergeant major and battalion gunner. They all came in and immediately asked the SNCO what the hell was going on. Well, he kept tripping over his words and looking at me the whole time. The entire time these marines were in this firefight, this guy was on the phone smoking a cigar. They looked at my map where I had everything plotted and I briefed them on the situation. They were really impressed with the entire set up. Of course, again, it got me on the radar of the higher ups, but consequently called me out to my peers.

One morning, a few weeks before that incident, I made my instant coffee trying to make it a normal day. I walk into the COC and saw that the sat phone wasn't being used. I grabbed it and went to call my sister. One thing every family member or loved one needs to do for someone deployed is to always answer the phone when you see a foreign number. I grab the phone and walk to the only semi-private place we had on that patrol base. As I walk, there is a low point in the dirt mound we have as a protection wall and I see a convoy in the near distance. I dial her number and it rings and rings and goes to voice mail. I leave a message and say that I'll try back in a few hours. The very second I hit end on the phone, I hear, feel and see one of the largest explosions to date. All I could think was, "Ah fuck, the convoy." For a second, I thought I could have set off the IED with the sat phone. I run to the COC to see what's going on. Two marines and myself get the GBOSS on this convoy. It was route clearance and the lead vehicle got hit. You could see two people with the detectors doing their sweeps, then a second IED goes off and you see a red dust cloud. Not 30 seconds later a third goes off on the other side and another red cloud emerges. We immediately send out a foot QRF. After four days in river city, I got to call my sister back who was a little worried because when I said I would call back, it usually didn't take 5 days. I made something up, like we got busy or something. This wouldn't be the last time our platoon saw these types of clouds and when I got back to the states, these images would contribute to many sleepless nights.

The constant attention from senior officers and SNCOs on how impressed they were about how well I did my job and the word the senior staff got back from my home unit always made me resent myself a little. Yes, that's all good and well, but I really didn't care about that crap. All I cared about was doing my job the best I could to help and make sure that all of us came back. We were very lucky in the fact that everyone in my platoon did come back. We had a few purple hearts given out, but all us came back with all of our limbs. The biggest part of my post-traumatic stress was the fact that I felt I could have done more. That I should have done more. The resentment I felt towards myself when my own lieutenant was telling our platoon that I'm not going on very many foot patrols because my "job" was more valuable than theirs was completely ridiculous. The resentment I got and should have gotten with a mentality like that lieutenants, made me feel like I wasn't a part of this group of great men, when all I've tried to do was do my job. There were many times I talked to my lieutenant about this until I got into a heated conversation and he told me about a promise he made. He was good friends with that battalion FAC I was the RO for during the work up. They talked when I got picked for 3rd platoon. The FAC made my lieutenant promise him that he would do anything to make sure that I made it home. To lower the risk, I didn't go on foot patrols. The even sadder part, was about a week after we got home, I got a phone call from the FAC.

"I heard you turned into a homo. Is that true?" he asked.

This caught me very off guard and I stumbled and lied saying of course not, but you could tell in my voice that I was lying through my teeth.

"That's very disappointing," he said, and hung up. I haven't heard from him since.

He was one of the reasons why I couldn't do all the parts

of my job and put a lot of unneeded stress on my lieutenant. When he found out I was gay, I was out with the trash. My platoon found out I was gay while deployed by a video I had on my iPod that I completely forgot was on there. I got back from replacing broken radios from the main Camp in our area of operation. When I got back, I went to put my shit away and saw the grenade crate I used as a foot locker was messed with. I check and saw that my iPod was missing, which really isn't a deal at all. People borrowed it all the time, but this time who ever had it, went through the videos. It was such a rookie mistake. People borrowed this iPod all the time and I didn't even think twice about it, because I had no idea the video was even on there. Well, this turned me into a very easy target. There was already resentment towards me, because the way you proved yourself was the number of foot patrols one went on. I was already barred from going on most foot patrols. It was such a deal that at the end of the deployment there was a tally on who went on the most and least foot patrols. Surprisingly, I wasn't the one who went on the least. Nevertheless, now that the rumor mill has spread like wild fire I was constantly called out. I never really admitted I was gay and as this was happening in country, back in the states "don't ask, don't tell" was getting repealed. Ironic, no? Now that it's out, but not officially admitted by myself, I was still an easy target for misplaced anger towards the fact that I wasn't allowed to go on these patrols or that my "job" was "more important." I got a lot of threats. I got called out and the view of myself by a lot of marines turned dark. I got death threats.

"I can't wait till you do go on a patrol. You better watch your back, you faggot."

I took these things in stride, telling myself it was just misplaced anger from the stresses of war that we are all going through. I continued to do my job and tried my best to not let these comments affect anything. I did well in country, but when I got back home... it was a completely different story.

I got back from war and I didn't handle it very well. I would say half of my issues were from the combat I saw, but the other half being that my brothers from war now wanted nothing to do with me. It felt like I was the trash we threw in the fire pit. The times we were up for days, all the missions, operations, stupid fuck-fuck games seemed to mean nothing. We had a month-long stand-two order, which means for every post that only had one marine in it, now needed to have two marines. We were already extremely undermanned, which meant no one slept for days.

I personally felt the second they found out I was gay, that brotherhood went down the drain.

When we went back to the states we had a two-week debriefing period in California before we got to finally fly home. The day I got home, I went to my grandparents' house. My extended family was there with huge smiles on their faces. I'm finally home and I sit and can only think, "I made it home." I hadn't been home for a day and they were asking questions. They wanted to hear stories. I was just looking out the window at the grass. I got my laptop out and started going through pictures of the marines I spent the last 6 months with. I show them marines I've only just met 6 months ago and wondered if I will ever talk to them again after how we left each other. We sat around the dining room table at my grandparents' house. My grandfather sat in a chair in front of the laptop while my uncle sat to the left and me to right. My father sat behind my grandfather. We go through pictures of the patrol base. I explain how we didn't have running water, we shit in bags and threw them in the fire pit and we didn't get to shower for three months. They were surprised, but it seemed like none of them had a real concept, except one; my grandfather. I looked at him and we had the same expression that neither of us really wanted to go through this. I just got back and the last thing I wanted to do is relive the hell I just went through.

We went through a few more pictures and then one came up on a dead mangled body of a Taliban member who got blown up when trying to set an IED overnight. I saw it and clicked passed it quickly. It took all of us off guard. Well, of course everyone wanted to look at it. The women walked away and the guys wanted to see the picture. At this point my grandfather didn't want to see it, got up and went into the other room. I wanted to do the same thing, but of course I got a million questions about it. Then it hit me. This is just a picture to these people, but a memory for me. After every conversation I had with Jack and the Vietnam Captain and my own brother... I finally got it. They were just conversations. They were amazing "war hero" stories to me before, but now they are memories.

When we first got back to California during that two-week debriefing period before we flew home, I was pulled aside by an SNCO from my original company who I thought very highly of. We sat down and he heard everything our platoon went through. We had a very real conversation about what he saw happen after the 2005 deployment. He went into detail and asked me to please not go down that road. I told him I wouldn't and I had the best intentions to not self-medicate with drugs or alcohol. Fast forward about two months, I'm not sleeping well and just in a bad place overall. With that conversation echoing in my head, I made an appointment with the local VA. A month later I got into the VA.

After about 15 minutes of talking to a doctor, she gave me a two-month supply of an anti-depressant and tried to give me a two-month supply of Vicodin to hold me over till the next time I could get an appointment.

I refused to take that strong of a pain medication and just asked for 800mg of Ibuprofen. I asked about seeing a psychiatrist and she responded, "Let's see how this works first." At that point I was done with the VA. I then paid out of pocket and saw two different psychiatrists. After three appointments each, they both told me the same thing. "I just don't think I'm the right person to handle these issues. Have you tried the VA?" I told both of them what happened with the VA pushing drugs and how it was months behind on getting veterans appointments. At this point I was done.

I started to drink heavily. It was the only thing I thought at the time that would let me sleep through a night and in the end, that's all I wanted. I would go out or get drunk every single night for about seven months. When you're angry, stressed and have high anxiety but want to think you're fine, adding alcohol into the mix can cause a lot of problems. At that time, I was dating a guy that was a bartender at the best gay bar/club in the city and that didn't help my situation. I would stay there till he closed every night he worked and when he didn't work, we usually ended up there at some point. We got into an argument one night and got into the car. I was drunk as shit and so mad that I punched his windshield hard enough that it cracked into a spired web. I don't know what it was about breaking glass, but when I was drunk and angry I loved breaking it. I went through new phones almost every month. I was living with my brother and thank God I had him. If it wasn't for him, I have no idea where I would be right now. He completely understood the anxiety, anger and rage I had.

We lived on a farm at the time, and someone had said something to me at a bar that completely set me off. When I got home, I was in a complete rage mode. He tried his best to calm me down, but something had to break. I threw my phone and completely shattered it, but that wasn't enough. We were out front and I was standing next to a window that looked over the patio. I turned and put my fist through it. My brother wrapped up my hand and I passed out somewhere. In the morning, I felt like the biggest piece of crap. He didn't deserve dealing with this. I hated the fact that I acted like that and after that night, I knew I had to change. I had become the person my Gunny pulled me aside and asked me not to be. I decided to try the VA again, but a different one. The first time I walked into this new VA, I saw a physiatrist. He worked with me for a few months and I found a more productive way to handle my feelings. I started sleeping through the night without having to get wasted and I came to terms with myself. I wanted to go back and tell my lieutenant to put me on more patrols, that his little promise does not apply to the laws of war and how much I felt that I could have done more while deployed for my platoon. I couldn't though. What's done is done and there is no changing it. I was very lucky that everyone in my platoon made it home with no major injuries. It was time to focus on my future and well-being.

This "disorder" is not a disease. It's a scar and before it becomes a scar it is an open wound. If you're bleeding, you ask for treatment, you treat the wound, clean the wound and don't cover it up pretending like it's fine. Just like post-traumatic stress, but after a while you must take off the bandage. You let the scar be seen to all. It doesn't matter what branch you served in or how much or little combat you saw. We all are connected by the brotherhood of the military. It doesn't just cross branches, but generations of war. We saw it in our grandparents during WW2, our uncles or fathers during Vietnam and now in ourselves when we look in the mirror each day. It is something we learn to live with each and every day and try to make it better for the next generation to come.

A WARRIOR'S GHOST
"Pitch"

Pitch served in the Navy on SEAL Team 5. His story shows us how to lean on the right people and how to be the one others need to lean on.

I would like to start with a little background on myself, my time spent in the Navy and situations I experienced in combat zones. I joined the Navy when I was nineteen. I spent most of my time on ships working on F18's as a plane captain and did not see any action. During this time, I did deploy three times on aircraft carriers. About seven years into my career I decided I wanted to become a Navy Seal. The process you go through is grueling, to say the least, and took a great toll on me in order to succeed. My training put me in many difficult situations in which I had to learn to adapt and find solutions. My first tour to Iraq with my team was in 2006. Iraq was having presidential elections and we were doing the PSD (personal security detail) for the five candidates. It was an interesting deployment. I got to travel all over the country when the guy we were protecting traveled to meet and speak with the people. I got to work with some really great Marine and Army units as well as some foreign units. I really enjoyed working with the Polish GROM (special operations force). We spent four months in Iraq and finished out the last three in Guam where we did cross-training with foreign units. It was good training and interesting to see how other units operated. I got to work with the Korean special forces and the Singapore and Thai soft units. I did not come under any fire during this deployment, or engage the enemy.

My second deployment was also in Iraq, but a bit different than my first. This deployment was seven months of direct action and over-watch missions (the team would sit in a spot for a few days and watch an area). I also saw some Abrams tanks in action. Most of the over watches ended in a hot extract. They would come in and lock the area down for extract. I remember being at a local combat outpost and taking mortars and some gunfire. This was my first time experiencing combat. The whole thing lasted maybe a minute and a few local police were injured. We had two guys go down about a month into our deployment. Just two days before we were leaving to head back to the States, we had another guy go down. Some stray rounds came into the compound from the other side of the river, behind our compound. My buddy, who went on multiple ops, had been shot at, had rockets fired in his direction, among other things, walked out of his hooch (shelter) to throw away some trash while dressed only in his brown t-shirt, black shorts and flip flops, was hit by one of those stray rounds in the chest. He had to be rushed to the hospital to get worked on. The round went into his chest and through his lung and lodged into his spine. He ended up pulling through. He is fine now, but has a 7.62 round permanently lodged in his spine. It was too close to the nerves to get taken out. While my buddy was at the hospital getting worked on, the rest of the guys spent the next hour or so clearing the compound. It was common to hear gunfire and explosions every day. It actually was not normal if you didn't hear it. Mortars could hit at anytime and anywhere.

My last deployment was to the Philippines. This was a quiet one compared to the second deployment. I worked with the Philippine equivalent to the Seals, NAVSOG, for six months. They were fun to work with and I made some really good friends while working with them. I also spent about a month on an island in the south with the Army Special Forces guys. Our team did mostly humanitarian work that trip. We did a lot of MEDCAPS (Medical Civil Action Projects), trying to help improve the living conditions for the locals. We worked closely with the Army to help improve local schools and hospitals, getting local villages water. Though this was a relatively quiet deployment, there was one instance where things got a little dicey. We were doing a MEDCAP when our SBT (Special Boat Team) and a few of our team guys were dropping off some

116

nurses on one of the islands close by. When they were about two-hundred meters from the pier, six guys opened fire on the boat. The SBT guys were on top of it and got the boat out of the area in just a few seconds. No one ever expected that to happen. This just goes to show that no matter how docile the environment is, you always have to be ready. You hope for the best and expect the worst.

When considering what PTSD means to me, my initial reaction was to say that I did not have PTSD. But, once I started to discuss it with my wife, and she coaxed me to talk about experiences I have had, I began to realize that my reactions to certain situations might be an indicator that I do have some form of the disorder.

When I was living in Dallas four years ago, I was with a good friend of mine, Clint, who was also on Seal Team 5 with me for a time. We were at the Navy vs TCU football game in Texas and they were having Navy skydivers jump onto the field to open the game. We were getting the field ready for the jumpers, taking wind readings, monitoring wind speed and direction. When we were all set and waiting for the game to start, we started walking out of the tunnel and onto the field. We were coming out next to one of the end zones. To my right was a grass berm that went around the entire end of the field. I was busy watching what was going on out on the field and didn't notice the cannon that was on top of that berm. As Clint and I were walking, we were in the middle of a conversation and the cannon went off. I just about went face first into the dirt. I realized what was going on, looked over at Clint and saw him almost on his knees laughing at me. It was pretty funny. I started laughing myself and carried on with what we were doing, but my initial reaction was to drop down and take cover.

Another time I was in a grocery store and I was caught off guard by a loud bang. I dropped down to a knee and looked around. I realized the stock boy had knocked over an empty pallet. Once I realized what it was, I was fine, but again, my initial reaction was not what is considered normal.

There was another instance when I was living in Dallas

with my cousin. I was in my room playing my guitar with my headphones plugged in, so I didn't hear him come in the room. As I was playing I looked over and saw him standing there. My initial reaction was to grab the neck of the guitar and bring it back like a baseball bat to take a swing. I realized it was him and put the guitar down. We laughed and started talking.

Before I joined the military and even in the early part of my career, I never really thought about PTSD much. In part, because I really didn't understand it or know what it really was. Once I got to the Seal Teams and deployed a few times and noticed a difference in my behavior at home, I started asking questions and paying attention. But I still didn't really think about it too often. I thought some of the stuff going on was just a normal everyday thing coming back from a deployment. Plus, I was functioning normally. I didn't have trouble sleeping, I wasn't depressed, I wasn't having nightmares, no panic attacks or feeling nervous in crowds. None of the things you read about when reading about PTSD.

I never really thought about it until I got off of active duty and into the reserves. That is when I started seeing my actions in certain situations, so I started to read about it. While I was on active duty I asked a doc one time, "Why am I jumpy at home and not so much on deployment?" What made me ask this was while on one of my deployments to Iraq, me and the boys were watching a movie and there was a real big explosion close to our compound. It was big enough to make the door swing open to our hooch. We didn't think much of it. We just looked at each other, closed the door and went back to the movie. So, I asked...

"Why do I act like that while I'm overseas and when I'm home I'll almost drop to the floor when I hear a loud noise?"

I was thinking to myself, "Is this normal? Is this what PTSD is?" It was explained to me like this: When you're overseas in a combat zone, an explosion or gunfire isn't out of the ordinary. It's almost expected to happen, so you're always in some sort of state of readiness. When you're home, it's not normal, so your state of readiness is lower. But, it's that kind of thing that conditions my fight or flight instinct and causes me to react a certain way and initially interpret a situation. Basically, a loud bang on deployment is usually bad, so when I am caught off guard by a loud bang at home, my fight or flight instinct kicks in and my initial interpretation is, *"That's bad."*

Everyone is different and is affected in different ways. Some people's first instinct is to run, while others are conditioned to be more aggressive because that's what they know when a stressful situation occurs. I have become a very light sleeper. Most noises wake me up and I have been known to grab my gun and clear the house in the middle of the night after being woken up.

When I started to talk to my wife about this topic she had her own insight. She told me that there have been occasions where I was asleep and as she went to wake me, I was startled and woke with my fists raised. Since then, she has developed the habit of calling my name before she approaches the bed. She also noticed that when we are out on a walk, I will avoid the drain covers and walk around them. This is something I just subconsciously do, and seems normal, but to her it is a strange action.

In regards to PTSD and the different levels of severity, I feel that mental toughness plays a part in it, too. Not all people are geared to handle the stresses of a combat zone including people in the military. Everyone in a stressful situation will interpret that same situation differently. For example, a reporter will interpret a stressful situation differently than a military person. Everyone has a breaking point; some can handle more than others, depending on what type of training they have had and what state they are in mentally to begin with. Put a SEAL and a civilian in combat and the mental after-effects will probably be less for the Seal than the civilian because the Seal has been more mentally conditioned and prepared to handle the situation. I think this is why I may have milder reactions to situations, where someone else may not be able to handle it as well and will have more severe reactions.

My brother is a good example of having more severe reactions. He was never in the military but when he was younger he was a pizza delivery guy. One day some guys called to order a pizza and gave an address to a house no one was living in, in a cul-de-sac. He was severely beaten up by four guys and robbed. He was hit in the back of the head with a pipe or something which gave him a concussion and broke his nose. He was in the hospital for a few days. Shortly after that, the symptoms started to appear. On multiple occasions, he has had panic attacks, depression and anger issues. He doesn't work and is still living at home. He gets really uncomfortable while in big crowds. One time, he was driving home from the store and his car broke down. He had to pull over to the side of the road and ended up having a panic attack. He curled up on the floor and waited for the symptoms to pass. When they passed, he got out of the car and started to bang on people's doors saying he needed help until someone called the police. This has happened on a few occasions. He drinks quite often as an escape. This is one of the more severe reactions that I've seen.

In my job as a security contractor, I work with a lot of ex-military. Most of them have been in combat situations. I have had two guys I became friends with over the years commit suicide. I noticed some of the guys don't show as much and some are more obvious. One of those friends I worked with... you would never know he was suffering from PTSD. I spoke with him the day before he killed himself and he seemed perfectly normal. He was in high spirits and like his normal self. My brother on the other hand, you can tell just by looking at him that something is not quite right.

Because my reactions seem so mild, if visible at all, to me, it is hard for me to even see that I may have PTSD. Yet, when I talk with other people, they say that some of my reactions to situations and mannerisms lead them to think that I do. Because of this, I can see where there is a grey area that might lead to people going undiagnosed and untreated. I personally feel that I do not need any type of treatment and that the small "ticks" I have, do not interfere with my daily life. I also feel that there is another side to this coin as well. There are many who do not have symptoms, or signs, but choose to falsely get diagnosed with PTSD by playing up potential symptoms in order to get discharged, or disability, and take advantage of the system. In my opinion, this only makes it harder for the ones that legitimately do have PTSD to get diagnosed and get the help they need. I also think that a strong support system plays a big role in how someone handles PTSD.

I have a spouse that encourages me to express how I feel and also is a good outlet for talking about things if I feel the need. Many people do not have this and I think it is a factor in stressors building up without an outlet that can potentially exacerbate PTSD symptoms. I also have family to bring to light any strange behavior they might see that I would normally not see myself. I think that if you do not have people in your life that can see what you cannot, PTSD symptoms can go untreated and without getting the help they need, people can continuously get worse.

Over the years, I have seen many different levels of PTSD, ranging from no symptoms you can notice (like myself), to the extreme where they cannot take it any longer and take their life. In many cases (myself included), they do not think that they have PTSD, or if they do, it is a very light form. I think that it all comes down to how you handle your situations and if you get help when needed. I think that though I have seen many things, I have been able to deal with them and lead a normal life.

CHALK THREE

This last group were all members of the same unit in the United States Army; predominantly of Crazy Horse Troop, but all were of the Warhorse Squadron in the 3rd Stryker Brigade Combat Team, 2nd Infantry Division based out of Fort Lewis, Washington.

Though some deployed with the unit at different times, they often deployed together. Most of them know each other well. Most of them have experienced the exact same events.

All of them have different point of views on their deployments, firefights and other events. Their time spans from the creation of the first ever Stryker Brigade and deployment from 2003-2004 in Iraq, to a deployment during the height of the Iraq war including "The Surge" from 2006-2007, to the quietest time in Iraq from 2009-2010, to the unit's first deployment to Afghanistan from 2011-2012.

THE WEIGHT

John Francisco

     Even though we were given a packing list that covered the A, B, C duffel bags, ruck sack and assault pack, in the end, the weight of each soldier's gear is different. I'm not talking about the extra socks, porn, or the bags of candy which don't even last to the plane. I'm talking about the consciousness of our individual past. In our first deployment, we all took the required gear in the allotted bags, but we also learned, witnessed, and felt some things. As in other areas of life, some were good memories and some were bad. When the time came for the second deployment, we again packed our bags with the required gear, but our pack was heavier.

     We didn't take anything extra as the first deployment helped us understand what was necessary and what was ridiculous. Instead of our shoulders carrying the weight, our minds held a lot of the last go-around. We remembered what it was like to live through the shock of our first IED (Improvised Explosive Device) or how a car bomb could change people's lives forever. We remembered the electronic beep of radio comms (communications equipment) when our friends frantically relayed contact with the enemy or chasing phantom mortar echoes while the FOB (Forward Operating Base) lit up like the Fourth of July, just 300 meters away. We remembered a friend having the top of his Kevlar chewed by a sniper and wondering when it was our time to go. We remembered waking up to learn a friend had committed suicide or a member of the squadron was killed on one of the last patrols. We remembered driving down an urban road at night while receiving single shots from multiple buildings, listening to the ping off the armor, wondering when one was going to find its mark. We remembered rolling up on a kill house or on a group of decapitated local nationals and wondering how individuals could turn so violent against their own countrymen. We remembered meeting a dog handler and German shepherd at a meeting, only to have her taken the very next day. I remember waking up in a hospital, asking where I was and then screaming to be sent back. The doctors denied my request, the tears and guilt broke me. On top of the memories, in our following deployments, we had advanced in rank and position. We were not only responsible for ourselves, but we had to try and bring everyone back alive. Watching our leaders, friends, and subordinates kiss their wives and children goodbye filled us with an anxiety to ensure they reunited a year from now. Some unlucky souls were unable to fulfill the silent promise we all made to ourselves. Some of us added a little more weight to the next deployment. We didn't take any extra gear, but again, the weight was heavier.

Before I begin, I would like to explain my personal interpretation of Post-Traumatic Stress Disorder (PTSD). It cannot be summed up with a universal explanation. As with life, this designator has grey area. You will not be able to use my experience as a blueprint for management. All I ask, is for you to realize every single person on earth is hurting. That's every single person, military and civilian. That's all life is; you only get so much happiness. You have these little nuggets of pleasure and then these vast deserts of pain and agony. Many of us have buried the pain successfully, but just understand, no one smiles all the time. It's up to you to try and do your best... and remember it goes by fast.

To properly discuss the details of my experience we have to start at the beginning, which was late in 2002. I, like many young men at the time, joined the military for a simple reason: we knew a war was beginning and we were hungry for adventure. Does this make me selfish? I suppose so, but it served as an important driver. I chose Infantry because I knew it would have the best opportunity for what I believed would be an exploration of the world and myself. The decision served me well as I've been able to see a lot of the world in both peace and combat. I've had emotions and trials that have etched themselves into my soul, again, both in peace and combat.

For a very long time I denied having even the slightest suspicion of PTSD because I came up in the military learning that admitting to PTSD meant you were weak and untrustworthy. That was the thought of my generation; this war was new and we were just relearning its effects on soldiers.

There were a few moments in my first deployment that will hopefully stay with me forever. I say hopefully because they were exactly why I joined... the rush I desired. I was extremely lucky with my duty location and I honestly couldn't have had a better group of guys or unit. When I took leave and headed back home, all I could think of was getting back to Fort Lewis and being with my troop, "Crazy Horse." In all honesty, during my first deployment, I believe we could have accomplished anything. No mission was out of our grasp. When we first arrived in Kuwait, we waited the allotted time to cross the border into Iraq. I was a Private First Class with less than a year in the military.

I honestly thought we were going to get into a firefight the minute we crossed the border. That experience taught me that in war your brain can be the worst enemy. Everything was relatively calm as we travelled up to Samarra which was our first mission. We were set to clear the massive city of insurgents. I remember the night we approached the city and my platoon sergeant had just fired in the vicinity of some individuals acting suspiciously in a trash field. No one could confirm their actions but no one was taking any chances. Keep in mind, this was 2003 which meant it was the Wild West in Iraq and anything and everything went. I remember approaching Samarra with night vision and can still recall two streams of tracer fire crossing each other like the cross sabers in Baghdad. I looked up and a C-130 Specter Gunship lit up a target on the outskirts of the city. I remember thinking this is what I wanted, only a handful of individuals have observed scenes like this. Later in the day we received enemy contact and a Stryker was immobilized; a friend of ours was injured and had to be evacuated out of theater. Whenever you lose anyone, regardless of being killed or injured, it affects you. Your brain starts wondering if that soldier is going to make it and what he will do in the future, but then you begin wondering if you will be the next to fall. We all believe it will never occur, until it starts happening around you.

After the Samarra operation, we went to a place called Hatra and an Iraqi ammunition dump we referred to as the "gold and silver mines." It was a huge depot where Saddam Hussein kept a portion of his armory. We were tasked with defending the location while EOD (Explosive Ordinance Disposal) teams destroyed the munitions. The items within the depot weren't just 7.62 small arms and RPG's (Rocket Propelled Grenades). It also included air-to-air missiles and heavy artillery. One good memory about the first deployment was the disposal of that 80 tons of munitions. We had all climbed onto the roof in order to observe the "fireworks" and we were expecting a show. It was raining that day and we were listening to the countdown on the net.

"Three, two, one," and an explosion occurred that I can't describe.

Another thing that sticks out from that day is the reaction to the rain. As it was falling the compression wave from the explosion pushed the rain away from the blast expanding in a bubble. It kept climbing upwards, away from the blast. At its apex, it broke and the rain continued on its path to the earth. It is still one of the most amazing things I have ever witnessed.

I also have a memory of being in a makeshift Moral Welfare and Recreation site using the internet. I heard a faint explosion outside the camp and didn't pay it much attention, but then another sounded, followed by another. By the time the third hit, I was out the door, on the way to our Command Post/Barracks. We had two platoons in the middle of hostile territory and if the insurgents wanted to, they could take us. I ran into the barracks and everyone was grabbing weapons and gear, so I naturally thought we were being overrun. I honestly thought I was going to die that night. I took my kit, ran outside, took cover under a Stryker and waited to engage anything deemed hostile. As I lay there, I could see silhouettes in the distance. They appeared just outside the wire, running back and forth. I saw an explosion to my 12 o'clock. It was a mortar round impacting about 100 meters out. A few seconds later, another mortar exploded 50 meters to my front. I then realized what they were doing. They were walking/adjusting the rounds in on our position. I stayed under the Stryker waiting for the third and possibly final mortar to hit... and then it did. It landed about 25 meters to my left and had deviated ever so slightly, saving my life. The explosions slowly expired, as did the small arms and moving silhouettes, but I quickly realized that I was in control of nothing here.

We later moved to Mosul and got acquainted with the term "presence patrol." It's basically a polite way to say, "drive around until you get shot at." I was slotted as a gunner on our Stryker, but one day I was asked to drive. Our convoy was traveling down a major traffic artery of the city when we were engaged by a VBIED (Vehicle Borne Improvised Explosive Device or "car bomb"). The memory has about expired except for a letter I wrote to a friend that got injured in the blast. I do remember sitting in the drivers' hole and being washed over in noise, heat and the feeling of a vacuum as fire consumed the air around the Stryker. Time seemed to slow down in that moment as it would in future engagements. I could hear the members on the Stryker scream out as we were engulfed in flame. The .50 cal gunner, Baker, lost an eye and rear gunner, Lynch, received burns on his face and hands. I remember talking to the rest of the convoy after we made it back. They said after the initial blast they couldn't see our Stryker, then it appeared like a ghost ship out of the fiery, black smoke. We had no signs of life except for the slow movement forward. The VBIED had flattened nine tires on the Stryker, to include the spare on the roof. Regardless, I followed the convoy up the road, where we could assess the casualties. However, as the medics dismounted, the insurgents engaged us with small arms fire. Rounds echoed and ricocheted off the street and vehicles. We were forced to remount and head back to base. Another friend was evacuated. Yet again, your mind starts playing with you.

Your personal life also plays with your head when you're deployed. Being deployed can make you forget relationships, remember relationships, or even commit suicide. Our troop experienced all three of these events during our first deployment. Some guys would come home to a family that had moved on, and one would receive a "Dear John" letter, only to reply with a bullet. This incident hit the troop pretty hard because the individual was a friend who we drank with and became close to prior to deployment. I had no idea he was feeling the way he did. That is one of the reasons why, when they start preaching suicide prevention, I barely listen anymore.

Some people you can help, but if someone wants to go they will find a way, there's no denying it. I was selected as this individual's honor guard and I remember sitting outside with our M4's waiting to render our final three round salute. I remember standing at attention so long that my arm fell asleep and as they gave the command, "Ready," I had difficulty pulling the charging handle to chamber a round. In my mind, it appeared sloppy... a messy good-bye to a good friend. It's strange, but that's all I recall from our friendship.

Remembering relationships can give you a reason to continue, especially on days when you have had enough. I still had regular contact with my civilian life in the beginning years. It was still new enough where both worlds blended together. There was one person that always traveled with me from place to place. I don't know why I was unable to shake her from my memory, but that's how it goes sometimes. I met her in High School, which wasn't long before my first deployment. I remember sitting on a cot in the gold and silver mines reading a letter she had written me. I could faintly smell the perfume and just the appearance of the handwriting reminded me of her. I had these fantasies that I would make it home alive and I could have it all. I could have my military career and her; a perfect life. An illusion of youth, but it kept you going.

The rest of the deployment had its ups and downs. We had plenty of enemy contact, which equaled an abundance of adventures. We got to experience the business end of AK-47s, RPKs, RPGs, rockets, mortars, VBIED's and even an incident where we listened to the chemical alarms ring. We took anything and everything they could throw at us and kept coming. The insurgents even gave us a lovely nickname, "The Ghost Riders."

What's funny is I can remember the first day crossing the border, being afraid that I was going to be killed in the first five minutes and I remember the last day, where we were almost killed in the last five minutes. We had all boarded a C-130 about to leave Mosul, about to head back to the world of air conditioning and beer. We were packed into the C-130 like sardines, as usual, and screwing around, as usual. As the plane started to taxi down the runway an explosion erupted on the tarmac. We were getting hit in the very last minute of our deployment. The C-130 gained speed and felt like it shot straight up. When the plane didn't explode and we were airborne we were again laughing at the close call. We knew what it was like on the ground at that very minute and we didn't have to play the game anymore.

After a deployment, you go through a session of medical release to ensure you're stable enough for the civilized world, and then you're usually released for 30 days of rest and relaxation. Guys usually take this time to see what jail is like or to drink until they're covered in vomit. I traveled back to Virginia to visit my old life in Stafford. I got drunk with old friends, showed them the proper way to clear a room and decided to sober up for a day to take my sister, Tara, to the gun range. I remember walking with her up to the range and suddenly there was multiple shots. I immediately crouched and instinctively reached for an M4 that wasn't there. I collected my thoughts and laughed it off. My sister was concerned with this reaction. I shot with her at the range but that incident should have been an indicator that some of the war had followed me home.

I can remember sitting at home, watching the news in Iraq. Strangely, I missed the excitement and buzz of combat. A story came on about a suicide bomber hitting the chow hall in Mosul on FOB Marez. As I watched the story unfold I looked at the chow hall and saw where I had eaten daily. I had once again escaped death by an unknown coincidence. I don't consider myself a lucky individual but once you cheat death on multiple occasions, you start to worry if death will come looking for his due.

What's strange is when I got back I never followed up on reconnecting with my old girlfriend. You make many promises and plans while deployed and then you return and things get sidetracked or you ignore them. I wanted to see her but what was I going to say? I couldn't ask her to leave her life and join mine across the United States. It wouldn't be fair; it would be selfish. I figured it would be better to let her have her life and I would have mine. I wished it could be different but, again, that's how life is sometimes.

I spent the rest of my time with family on the east coast then headed back to Fort Lewis, Washington. I became a squad leader, which meant I had four guys to run a mortar Stryker. Life was simple in Washington State. We trained for another deployment and I attempted to master the skills necessary to be a squad leader in combat. I remember driving on Interstate-5, headed back to post and there was a pile of trash on the side of the highway. A pile of trash was a perfect place for an IED but I told myself I was back in the States, forget it. As I got closer, my speed increased, my grip tightened on the steering wheel and I gritted my teeth, awaiting the explosion. I passed the pile and nothing happened, I slowly began to catch my breath and relax. Maybe I forced myself to stay in the lane closest to the trash to prove everything was going to be OK, who knows?

In time, some of the old faces from the first deployment began to disappear, but the comradery of the troop was still strong. Another deployment was on the horizon and we were ready. The only issue that had changed was that I wasn't responsible for just myself anymore. I had to bring my four guys back home alive. I remembered from the first deployment that once you were on the ground you had no control of the events surrounding you. I was nervous that I would fail, that I would let a friend die. I had one friend named Bell and I was friends with his wife, Jen. I remember standing outside the squadron and we were saying our goodbyes and taking pictures. She approached me and asked me to promise to bring him home. I remember feeling like a jerk because I wouldn't do it. I couldn't promise that.

When we deployed the second time, we arrived in Baghdad to be a part of "the surge" in Iraq. Baghdad was a hot mess. Every other day you went out and discovered dead bodies. You were actually curious as to how in the hell this town could even be populated with so many deaths. I remember going through an area called trash alley that served as a makeshift morgue for the insurgents. We were rolling very slow to identify any bodies and to prevent any IED strikes. I remember a clearing on the east side of trash alley and noticed a bunch of dogs, so we went to investigate. Upon arrival, we found an arm sticking out of the ground that was being chewed on. After getting rid of the animals, we called the Iraqi Police to come and pick up their dead. We had to sit there and secure the bodies, making us a static target, as we waited to see if the

Iraqi Police were going to screw with us or not. They finally arrived and began to dig up the bodies. As soon as the corpse made contact with air, the worst smell I have ever had the pleasure of experiencing, engulfed us. Now, every time I smell anything decomposing I am reminded of that scene. A scene of Iraqi's digging up partially decomposed bodies out of the ground while the limbs broke apart due to the heat. It was a sight, to say the least.

During another experience in Baghdad, we approached a "kill house." A kill house was a location that insurgents would take LN's (local-national Iraqis) and torture them for information or for assisting American forces. We pulled up, secured the perimeter and sent a squad in to clear it. As soon as they entered the house they reported dead bodies. The bodies had been tortured with a drill and had marks into their temple's and groins. The squad pushed to the second floor. More dead bodies. They finally arrived on the roof, and when they appeared topside we received RPK machine gun fire from an adjacent roof. The gun trucks shifted to provide cover for the dismounted squad and luckily we got everyone back alive. With our dismounts out we had no ability to pursue this new contact, so we had to reload and try again later. I was always curious if the tip on the kill house was given by an LN for the sole purpose of ambushing an American patrol. That engagement made me curious about the intelligence process. Mainly because I thought Military Intelligence would be interesting, but partly because if it was some stupid private that sent us to an ambush, I wanted to ring his neck.

One incident in Baghdad stands out above the rest. It wasn't a typical engagement like the firefights we had before with small arms hitting the armor and street around you, followed by Apache's flying overhead attempting to identify targets. Strangely moments like that are chaotic for a moment and then they're over. This engagement took place one night on a street we called power line road. We were conducting a late presence patrol and everything was quiet. All of a sudden, a single shot echoed in the street. We waited for a follow-on burst of fire, but there was nothing. We slowed down to identify the shooter and another single shot rang out. We were travelling at a very slow rate down an open road while individuals were taking single shots attempting to hit one of our gunners or turret commanders. We continued down the street and kept receiving the single fire but couldn't identify the shooter. I was completely freaked out waiting for a round to make contact with my head and I responded by firing half a mag into an alleyway. The burst resulted in ending the single shots and allowed a much-needed release. The next day we were looking at our Strykers and there it was, an impact right on the periscope of the C53 vehicle. Three inches up and a very good friend wouldn't be here today. It wasn't the VBIEDs, IEDs, machine gun engagements, indirect fire or daily run-ins with dead bodies that scared the hell out of me. It was a group of guys taking single shots at our platoon late one night in Baghdad and I'll never forget it.

Late in 2006, we were conducting a night time patrol opposite FOB Falcon in Baghdad. It was a typical, quiet night and we were out "fishing" for contact. Suddenly, the faint noise of mortar fire came from an unknown location. We immediately switched into high gear attempting to locate the point of origin. Less than a minute after the shot, the FOB began to light up in a way that can't be explained to someone who didn't witness it. The insurgent mortar had hit the Ammunition Holding Area (AHA) and set off secondary explosions which resulted into cooking off of the entire AHA. Imagine, you hear the shots, you hear the Tactical Operations Center screaming into the net that the FOB is on fire and you're stuck in the middle of Baghdad, unable to provide the needed assistance. We drove around for an hour looking for anyone to kill, and no one was available. We realized after that lucky hit, the insurgents likely decided to celebrate behind closed doors. If we would have found them, it would have been an unholy payback. We had to go to FOB Union that night because we couldn't even drive on Falcon due to the unexploded ordinance littering the ground. Thankfully, all of our guys made it through that ordeal alive, and now they have one hell of a story.

You rarely remember random dates in life, but one is burned into my memory: January 28, 2007. It was the day that forced me in a different direction. A day that violently tossed me away from my old life and set me on a new path. We were conducting a presence patrol in Baghdad and, as usual, I was the lead vehicle. Suddenly a metal ting rang out on the Stryker armor.

"What was that?" I asked my gunner, Bell.
"I don't know," he simply replied.

A second later a grenade detonated beside us. We both took the explosion with varying degrees of injury. Bell received wounds to his hand, arms, and later to find out nervous system. My face and upper torso was lightly peppered with shrapnel with one tiny fragment entering my temple. Bell fell first and Compton, one of our dismounts, came to check on him. He screamed for our medic, Doc Williams, and then I fell. Doc hit Bell with some morphine and then attended to me. I asked how Bell was and Doc started to touch my face.

"Get off me," I said.
"You're bleeding," he replied
"Well then, get to work."

My crew saved our lives that night, raising hell to get us to the casualty support hospital (CSH). I have no doubt they would have done everything in their power to save us that night. That's the awesome thing about platoons in combat. When it gets serious, you will risk anything and everything for your team, there are no best friends or rivals. You take care of the team, end of story.

Just to drive this point home, and to relate how that last sentence means so much, I have to tell you a little back story. The guy who was driving when I got hit was named B-tyne. B-tyne had a drinking problem and was a thorn in my ass from day one. He was a great guy when he was sober, just a little testy. Anyway, he went on a bender one night and ended up AWOL (Absent Without Leave) from the troop. We had to inventory his stuff and I had to report him out of ranks day after day. He finally showed back up and I lit into his ass, knocking shit over, cursing him up and down. I was so mad I was shaking. He took the ass chewing and I went to work on chaptering him out of the Army. This was not the first time alcohol had played a factor in his performance. Due to the upcoming deployment, chaptering him out was a no-go. We deployed together and he did fine, due to the absence of alcohol. My point is this, he knew I tore into his ass, he knew I tried to chapter him out of the military and he still took it upon himself to drive to the CSH by memory, with no communications, at the fastest rate a Stryker could travel. Yes, he hit everything there was to hit in Baghdad on the way, but Bell and I are alive because of his actions. I never had a chance to say it to the group, but to the crew of C51, I can never repay you for what you did. You saved my life and I am forever in your debt.

Doc Williams later told me, that after I was hit my brain started to swell. My speech and memory declined as we travelled down the road. I couldn't recognize my own squad after a 15-minute cruise in Baghdad. They got me off the Stryker and took me in the CSH where I'm told a preacher read me my last rights as they emplaced a temporary shunt to release the pressure off my brain. I have no recollection of this, the only knowledge I have of that night in Baghdad are from pictures and drunken stories of friends.

My very first memory in the United States was of my grandmother Viola standing over me. I could remember it because the light was shining through her grey hair. I had no idea where I was or what I was doing. My brain was scrambling to reset the processes of thought, speech, and movement. One function that was causing trouble was an issue with my hippocampus, the gland that regulates your body temperature. As my body was resetting, my core temperature would shoot up to 100 + degrees, requiring the application of ice packs. As I laid there shivering, my core temperature would say, "OK," and drop to the low 90's requiring a heating blanket. We played this game for a few days. I was in the Intensive Care Unit as they combatted sessions of Code Blue and Code Brown. My mother told me I was travelling the world daily.

"John, do you know where you are?" she would ask.

Some days, I'd be in the hospital, sometimes Iraq and occasionally I'd be back in Virginia. My mother and sister stayed with me as much as possible, visiting every week and unfortunately for them, I was unable to retain any memory of their previous visits. Due to this lapse, they had to sit through multiple viewings of Borat and Elf.

My injury was a penetrating head wound, classified as a Traumatic Brain Injury. As I slowly began to regain my consciousness, I discovered I had lost the ability to walk, talk, or use the bathroom as a normal person. I had to relearn everything. At the time this was devastating. I had gone from a fully capable Infantry squad leader to an invalid stuck in a bed. In Bethesda Medical Hospital, I broke down and cried because I was unsure if I could reclaim what I had lost. Friends would come to visit me from my life before the military and I was embarrassed of my condition.

My memories of Bethesda, Richmond Veteran Affairs hospital, and Walter Reed are a blur. Only a few memories have stayed with me, but before I recall the events, I want anyone reading this to fully understand the situation. In every single hospital I received care, I was given everything I needed to succeed. If it was not for the dedication and professionalism of the therapists, doctors and nurses I wouldn't have made it. I can never repay these professionals but I would like to thank them for giving me my life back. I was lucky enough to find the doctor's office who emplaced the permanent shunt into my brain. I knew he was busy and I didn't want to take his precious time because he may have needed it to save another life. I just wanted to shake his hand, look him in the eyes and say thank you.

At the Richmond Veterans Affairs hospital, I remember walking down the hall being held up by a large male nurse who struggled with me each step of the way. I finally re-learned how to walk. I remember an attractive speech therapist who helped me stumble through each phrase until I was able to carry on a conversation. I also remember the devil, or occupational therapist, who had the job of re-teaching me my fine muscle skills. I had a sweet tooth in the hospital and she was aware of this. She also knew occupational therapy was the worst hour of my day. She gathered some change from her purse and said, "Here go to the vending machine and get something." It was difficult and embarrassing but I managed to put my 55 cents in for a candy bar. It isn't the gift I remember but a kind moment shared between two people, and hopefully I'll never forget her.

After about four months of rehabilitation and physical therapy, I was transferred to Walter Reed Hospital where I would be given a choice of medical discharge or the chance at a medical reclassification board. The military was and is all I've known in my adult life. It's like any career, some days are better than others, but I enjoy the challenges and adventures that are forced on me. I've been put into some situations that I can guarantee I wouldn't have chosen voluntarily. I was waiting in the hallway one day talking to another soldier who was waiting for his medical determination and we discovered we were both Infantry. We were both ground pounders that were in the wrong place at the wrong time. He turned to me.

"If I can't stay Infantry, I'm getting out."

I didn't reply, I just thought about what he said. I had to understand if I stayed in the military, my life as Infantry was over. A part of me would die but I could move on from my old life. Although I understood everyone in that ward had a choice to make, I wasn't done yet. He was called into the doctor's office and it felt strange being outside the door where an individual was voluntarily leaving the military. I spent the remainder of my time in Walter Reed receiving physical and mental tests to ensure I was capable of being retained by the United States military.

I was later discharged by the hospital and sent back to Fort Lewis. I was assigned to the rear detachment while our unit was still deployed and I was stuck with individuals awaiting disciplinary legal actions and brand new soldiers. Both cases serve as a pain in the ass for supervisors. I babysat the "Bad News Bears" for the allotted time, and counted the days until my guys came back. It was during this time I began drinking again. I drank a lot with my friends before we deployed, but now it was just me. Every weekend I would consume a case of beer alone, sitting in my living room watching TV. I remember one morning I received a call from work asking if I could take Staff Duty. I wasn't assigned this task but I said sure. For some reason, I drank especially hard the night prior and tempted the DUI gods by driving in early the next morning. The only reason this day sticks out is because I remember walking up to the Squadron doors and puking in the bushes. I felt like shit the entire shift.

Another night that sticks out was a Fourth of July when I was sitting alone in my apartment, again drinking heavily. I can't remember if I was thinking about the deployment or I was focusing on the fireworks. I sat there slowly turning up the TV because each small explosion was triggering a memory of small arms fire. I tried to make the memories stop with alcohol and with whatever was on the television but it crept back in my head. I just sat there stuck on my couch, full of fear as I listened to the explosions of the Fourth outside my apartment.

You may be curious on why I was alone so much after my troop redeployed home. They arrived back in the States and we met at their arrival on-post. I was so happy to see them, and they me. We may not have been married, but it was damn close. We said our hellos and I would stop by the troop every other day. I later got assigned to a Warrior Transition Brigade, where they decide if you're capable of being reclassified into another job. As I waited for this re-classification, I went back to school and stopped back by the troop from time to time. I missed everything about the squadron, the familiarity, my platoon, my job, my old life. I was and still am still friends with every single guy in the troop, but after my separation we began to drift apart. It's no hit on the guys; things were different because I was gone. It's just the way it is. It was time to move on but it was difficult to say goodbye to that life. I can honestly say after 13 years in the military, I have never found another group of guys like Crazy Horse. I'll never have brothers like I did in those days.

Being forced to re-class into a new Military Occupational Specialty felt like I was betraying my past. The Infantry world is ugly, but beautiful. You suffer the most through the actions of Mother Nature and whoever the enemy is that day, but when the pain is gone, you miss it. You miss the life and your friends. I chose to reclassify to Military Intelligence where I felt I could still make a difference in combat. I always thought it was weird for the medical doctors to say...

"You technically have brain damage, so Infantry is no longer an option. You can be Military Intelligence though."

With the green light, I successfully transferred to Military Intelligence and it served as a wakeup call. It is a different world entirely. I'm not saying that combat arms are any better than non-combat arms, they just have different worlds. It's a different setting, language, and behavior; changes I'm still adjusting to today. But I have a perspective a lot of my Intelligence brethren lack. It doesn't make me any better than anyone else, but I am able to translate intelligence into a tactical flavor.

I've been back to Iraq and Afghanistan as an Intelligence Analyst and even though it's difficult and exhausting, I enjoy working a problem set to give our guys the advantage they deserve. Today's enemy has learned to counter the most technologically advanced military on earth. It is challenging to stay ahead of their tactics and procedures, but if I hear my work benefitted the team, it's almost like the old days.

So, when I started this adventure, I joined as Infantry, I almost died in Baghdad, which eventually resulted in a transfer to Military Intelligence. This was simply an attempt to rejoin combat operations. After my tour in Afghanistan, I applied to become an All Source Warrant Officer. I failed the initial application and thought my goal was unattainable due to my injuries, but I tried again a few years later and was luckily accepted. Warrant Officer school was physically difficult due to my injury, but I made it. I am now fully involved in daily operations against the war on terror.

Many people ask me how I received my shunt and I tell them about dying multiple times, only to be brought back multiple times. They reply with the typical response of "Oh, I'm sorry," and I reply with "Well, at least I'm not in a box." In reality, I'm actually lucky. I was stuck in the trap in which we're all victim to. We become comfortable, and before we know it, the ride is over. Coming so close to death, I was reminded of how short of a time we actually have. Yes, it leads to some tired days or weeks but I'm trying to see as much as I can before it is time to punch out again. I'm older now and as I think about my life, I occasionally wish I would have chosen a different path. I wonder what it would be like to go to work at nine and get off by five. What it would be like to hear a family in the house, rather than silence? I wish I wouldn't have pushed relationships away; I wish I would have been braver. But maybe it's for the best, or at least that's what I tell myself.

People often ask if I have any issues or regrets with my choice. They usually end the questions with a "Thank you for serving." When I was younger, this bothered me because I didn't know how to respond. I wanted to give them the honest response of, "I didn't do it for you and I don't care about your pity, thank you." The reality of the situation is, when you're over there, everything Stateside is secondary. All we care about is our friends and doing everything we can to make sure they make it back alive. I can't describe what you feel when a friend is hurt or killed, but the loss stays with you. I've always said that a deployment is equivalent to an entire lifetime. In that year, you have so many emotional ups and downs, so many thoughts and wishes that an entire lifetime is compressed into 365 days.

Maybe that's why so many of us have a hard time showing emotion after a deployment. To a certain extent, we've learned to turn-off our feelings. Most of us learned it's best to concentrate on the mission. Just work on the here and now. If you begin to think, your thoughts will take you to a place you don't want to go. Like I said, your brain can be your worst enemy. In response to "Thank you for serving," I've learned to simply say "You're welcome." I now understand people are just attempting to show support, even though they and I come from two separate worlds.

I have friends that have left the military and they say they miss it. They don't miss the details, inspections, and occasional crap situations. They miss their brothers... they miss their family. I've spoken to retirees and they describe the same emotion. I honestly have no idea what I would have done if I was forced out, and that's probably why I worked so hard to stay in. I now realize that you never know what you're capable of until a situation is forced on you.

I recently went to Hilton Head with my sister and her husband during another Fourth of July. The night air was filled with explosions but I didn't sit in my room fearing the past. I took a beer outside and listened to the firework audibles bouncing off the hotel terrain and remembered what it felt like to be fully involved in urban operations. I closed my eyes and recalled the sounds of the Stryker and chatter of comms as we listened to explosions in the distance. I sat there and missed the excitement and brotherhood of combat, but all good things must come to an end.

This book is meant to give advice on PTSD and recommended ways to cope. As previously stated, every situation is not the same and every individual reacts differently to their past. I've successfully countered my experience by focusing on the future. All the events I've described are now simply memories. Perhaps I was blessed with a bad memory, or perhaps the reason I was able to leave the events in the past is a renewed focus on the future. The past is often a dangerous place to revisit, so you must remember that you have to remain committed to the present and future. You have to make goals and work very hard to see those goals come to fruition. Sometimes you will fail in life, but remember success consists of getting up just one more time than you fall. That may sound like a cheesy motivational poster but it's the truth. A truth that worked for me.

Insha'Allah

"Shep"

Before I joined the Army, I think the best way to describe me was... clueless and foolish. I figured I'd be able to just figure things out without any real structure. I was newly married and working as a painter for an ex-con because I had recently quit my union carpenter job. They wanted to drug test me and smoking weed was way more important than having a good job.

We were living in a shitty little apartment right outside the gate with an old console TV, a flea infested couch and a queen size air mattress. Life was awesome. That was until I went to cash my paycheck one day and found out my boss had emptied the business account and skipped town. I had no idea what I was going to do. My in-laws told my wife she could move back home but I couldn't go with her since I was a "loser pothead that would never do anything with my life." Luckily, she stuck to her guns and I was allowed to move in with my wife.

I didn't have a job. I didn't have a high school diploma; only a GED. I had no idea what I was supposed to do. The only person I had in my corner was my wife. We had previously discussed me joining the Army but now it was time to take a really hard look at it. I sat down and thought about why I had quit everything else I had ever tried to do. Whether it was high school, football, carpentry, or Denny's I always quit. I realized I quit because I could. There was nothing telling me I couldn't so when things got hard or I made up some random excuse about it being hard I would quit. I knew with the Army I couldn't do that. I couldn't just say, "Man, this blows. I'm outta here!" I knew I would have to see it through. I would be force-fed responsibility, even if it killed me.

Going through OSUT (One Station Unit Training) almost broke me! From day 1 I fought it. I was that asshole private that wanted to argue and got scuffed up for it... then argued some more. They fucked me up so bad one time I called my wife in tears telling her that I couldn't do it. I couldn't hang. IT was too much. In not so many words my 5'4", 100-pound wife told me to sack up and quit being a loser. It was actually kind of refreshing. No one, no one who really mattered anyway, had ever been straight with me like that. That was my wake-up call. From then on, I tried everything I could to be a good soldier. I finally had someone to be proud of me.

When I first got to Fort Lewis, Washington, in 1999, it was a rough start. I didn't get along with my TC (Truck Commander) at all and he would smoke the dog shit out of me frequently. Fortunately, my PSG (Platoon Sergeant) saw this conflict and switched me to a different section and I began to thrive. I started really enjoying the Army. My first 63-day field problem to Yakima kicked my ass, but in hindsight, I enjoyed it. Then it was off to NTC (National Training Center) to get certified for a potential deployment to Bosnia. As soon as we got back though it all changed. My heavy brigade was selected to transition to a new medium brigade. The next two years was nothing but vehicle training, dismounted field problems, turning in vehicles and drawing new ones. That taught me to really embrace the "big green weenie," as we called orders that came from "the man." I got promoted to E4 and was supposed to go to PLDC (Primary Leadership Development Course), but failed a height/weight test the night before. That was discouraging, but I knew I had the knowledge to still do my job whether I was 2% overweight or not.

On September 11, 2001, myself and few buddies were standing out by my car smoking cigarettes before PT (Physical Training) and listening to 106.1 FM trying to figure out the trivia question they were asking, "This gets stolen in the U.S. every seven seconds," when they broke in with a report that a plane had hit the WTC (World Trade Center) in New York City. We were shocked and tried to figure out how the hell a pilot could not see the building in his way. We went back to the trivia question when we heard about the second plane. That's when we knew something was definitely wrong.

We went off to formation and then a run. By the time we got back everyone was in panic mode. Another plane had hit the Pentagon. The president was calling it a terrorist attack and we knew our world had changed.

The next two years were a blur. Nothing but training. We got new vehicles. We did back-to-back NTC/JRTC (Joint Readiness Training Center) rotations; and by back-to-back, I mean some guys drove from NTC in the Mojave Desert to San Diego, loaded up Strykers on boats and got off in Louisiana while the rest of us went home for a week so we couldn't get family separation pay. Between NTC in California, JRTC in Louisiana, gunnery in Yakima, Washington, dismount lanes in the "back yard" (Fort Lewis area close to home), we had just less than 70 days off between January 2002 and November 2003. The rest of the time we were prepping for war.

I remember saying good-bye to my sons. I remember saying good-bye to my wife when she dropped me off at the Troop. I remember getting on the bus and myself and Ferguson, aka "Big Ferg," singing, "I'm leaving on a jet plane." We had this romantic vision of war; things we had seen on TV and movies. We felt invincible. We were United States Army Cavalry Scouts: the best MOS (Military Occupational Specialty) in the best Army on the planet. And we were going to mop up the pathetic remnants of the Iraqi Army. The same group of people that General Schwarzkopf wiped out in 100 days a decade prior. We got this!!

Mike Tyson once said, "Everyone has a plan, until they get punched in the face." Well, I imagine every soldier has a plan until they hear that first bullet whip past their head or that first mortar round lands on their checkpoint. Or, when you lose guys to a stupid accident. We prepped for every contingency we could as far as combat went but the first casualties our brigade sustained was due to a Stryker rolling over into a canal. We hadn't even had our first major mission yet and we lost people.

When we finally went into Samarra, we locked down that city so fast that the Iraqis started calling us "The Ghost Soldiers." We thought "Shit! This is easy." Then we lost a truck when it hit an IED (Improvised Explosive Device). The driver, Heyges, had a broken ankle but otherwise the only loss was the truck. The truck and our sense of invincibility. We weren't fighting the Iraqi Army. We were fighting the Iraqi people. We already knew not to trust anyone who wasn't in a uniform but now it just got confusing.

After Samarra, my deployment was pretty uneventful for the next six months. We moved from Samarra to Q-West, just south of Mosul. I was sent to HQ (Head Quarters) platoon with a First Sergeant who was more concerned about building a horseshoe pit and keeping his weapon clean than anything else. While the other platoons rotated through different areas, I became a "fobbit." TOC (Tactical Operations Center) shift, chow, gym, TOC shift, chow, bed. That was my schedule for six long months. Our troop had relatively little contact with the enemy at that time, but other troops in our squadron lost people. Good people that we all knew. It was shitty. Shortly thereafter, our troop lost a really great kid to suicide and another guy was sent back to the States after an attempted suicide. At the time, I couldn't understand why any of it happened. You assume someone is weak, mentally ill or just has demons that prevent them from wanting to go on but until you find yourself thinking about the same shit that's all you can do: assume.

I went on leave about that time and got to see my wife and kids. It was so great being back home, but different at the same time. The little bit I had seen outside the wire made me feel sketchy. I saw people in hijabs walking around and I started to glare at them because I couldn't understand why they were in my hometown. My leave happened during the Fourth of July so we went down to the waterfront to watch the fireworks. I just remember everything being fine watching that first firework go up and watching it go off. Then I felt it. I felt the concussion from the explosion and immediately went under the table. It scared the shit out of me! A couple people started laughing and that infuriated me, mostly because I was so embarrassed. I was a TOC Monkey. I had no right to be scared. I wasn't in the shit like everyone else. I admonished myself for being a bitch and got up to watch the rest of the show.

The rest of leave went off without a hitch and I got a plane to go back to Iraq a few weeks or so later. When I got to Kuwait, I ran into a couple guys from the unit and they told me that we had left Q-West and went to Anaconda outside of Ballad. When I arrived, I was told I had been moved from HQ to Raider Platoon (1st platoon). While I was disappointed I didn't get to go back to Bandit Platoon (3rd platoon), I was just happy to get the hell out of HQ.

My time with Raider was awesome! I got to go outside the wire and I felt like I was doing something. Like I actually earned the patch on my right arm. The schedule was rough and the heat sucked, but I felt like I was part of a team again. Not long after linking up with Raider we were told we were headed back north. After a brief stay in Tal Afar, we went into Mosul. That is when the shit hit the fan.

We lived in an area of the FOB affectionately known as "Mortar-ritaville," and it lived up to its name. It got to the point to where we didn't discuss whether or not we might get mortared on any given day, but how much and at what time. Same with contact outside of the gate: IEDs, mortars, random pot shots. Bandit platoon got caught in a substantial ambush one night and took some wounded. That's how the last few months went. We did have some fun though. We had poker nights and midnight chow for the last couple weeks after we signed our vehicles over to the unit relieving us. We had a couple more missions, though. Nothing too crazy until our very last one.

Our entire squadron went on a massive raid that was completely uneventful. On the way back, we were told not to go down Route Tampa because there was huge threat of IEDs. Most of us jumped on Route Toyota and made a bee-line back to the FOB. Unfortunately, one of the troops took Tampa anyway and on our very last mission we lost SSG (Staff Sergeant) Burbank while the gunner, Oreo, lost an arm. A truck filled with explosives slammed into the side of their Stryker and detonated. Three days later we were on a plane home. Three fucking days.

Coming home was surreal. I actually don't remember much about the time in between deployments. I remember having BBQs, parties and hanging out. I remember playing with my kids and moving to a new house. I remember being angry, flying off the handle if things were out of place, not sleeping and yelling at my kids because now I was angry AND tired. My wife told me that when I was tossing and turning one night she tried to calm me down and I punched her in the chest saying, "Get your fucking hands off me you fucking Haj!" I remember missing Iraq, the rush, the adrenaline that you got almost from just walking across the FOB some days. We had all been so turned up for so long that we couldn't just turn the shit off.

Whenever someone mentioned PTSD we either brushed it off or just called them a pussy. Everybody had bad dreams. Everybody drank a little bit more. It wasn't a big deal. I didn't think there was anything wrong with me. Most of us just chalked it up as part of the experience. We didn't talk about it. Mostly because we didn't want the label associated with it.

The ramp up for the second deployment was pretty much the same as the first one: training centers, Yakima, back yard, late nights and early mornings. This one was different for me, though. My wife, Heidi, was pregnant with our third child and it was going to be a little girl. I was finally getting "daddy's' little girl." Unfortunately, the deployment was scheduled for right around her due date so it added a bit of stress to an already stressful time. I lucked out though, and I was able to see her birth. Three weeks later, and on my son Sean's birthday, I left for my second deployment to Iraq.

One thing I will never forget about the Middle East is the smell. It's hard to describe. It's like a mix of rotting garbage, smoke, sewage and sweat. It permeates everything. As soon as I got off the plane in Kuwait, the heat smacked me in the face first and the smell hit me next. That's when I knew I was back in one of the most backward parts of the planet.

The second deployment was more violent than the first. More IEDs. More mortars. Random bodies showing up everywhere. The insurgency and sectarian violence was in full swing. You can actually see the difference between a body that dies of natural causes and one that dies a violent death. There is a hollowness to a violent death. It's like when someone dies peacefully in their sleep their soul has prepared to leave. But, when someone dies suddenly by having their tongue cutout and then shot execution style (a favorite method of the Jaysh Al Mahdi Militia or JAM), it's like the soul is ripped from their body. Like when someone moves out of a house versus abandoning it.

I think the biggest thing that bothered me was the apathy of the people around the violence. It was like they were almost immune to it. The straw that really broke the camel's back for me was when we were on patrol one day and were told to go check-out a body in one of the quieter neighborhoods in Abu Dashir. When we arrived, we found an old woman lying face down in a pool of blood, her groceries strewn about her. She had been shot in the back of the head by a sniper. Now, I'm not exactly sure what this old woman did to provoke a sniper to put a single round through her brain like he did. It could have been because she was a Christian or she might have been a Sunni in a predominantly Shi'ite neighborhood. Who knows? When we started asking people in the area why this may have happened they all responded with "Insha'Allah" or "if God wills it, it will happen." Every single one of these assholes basically told us that it was God's will that this old woman had to die such a violent and unnecessary death. Seriously? Are you fucking kidding me?! While I already my doubts about my own faith, this pretty much sealed it for me. What kind of perverse belief system would make all this violence and hate and ignorance OK? Not one that I want to be part of. More people have been killed in the name of God than any other reason in the history of man. More violence has been dealt out by people who believed it to be the will of God than any other purpose. "Wanna go to church?" Nah, I'm good.

After the second deployment, I was worried whether or not my daughter would even know me. When I left, she was three weeks old and while I came home for leave at the six month mark we had been extended to 15 months. I was coming home to a toddler, so I was pretty nervous. To my delight, she came right up to me, gave me a big hug and we have pretty much been inseparable ever since.

After we got home, the Armor Branch got wise to the fact that some of us had been at Fort Lewis for almost 8 years or longer so they sent us in all different directions. Luckily, I got Fort Knox and so did quite a few other guys. It was nice to be stationed with my brothers away from the OPTEMPO of deploying. We got together quite often and it was like a family. And boy, did we drink! We still didn't talk about PTSD. We still blew that nonsense off. To compensate for the lack of sleep and pushing everything deep down inside, we drank and got loud. Eventually we heard that some guys were having issues. Other people were talking to shrinks and taking meds. I think

149

what made me take a hard look at myself was when one of the guys I had looked up to almost my entire career, the guy who showed me what being an NCO (Non-Commissioned Officer) was all about, told me he was seeing a shrink. This guy was fucking steel. Nothing could phase this dude but he was going to see somebody. He was on meds. I was drinking and yelling at everyone over trivial shit. I made an appointment and went...once.

Shortly after that I got orders to go right back to Fort Lewis. Time to pack up and head back over the Rockies to God's Country. Right into a unit 136% strength on SSGs and prepping for Afghanistan. They made me the XO's (Executive Officer) gunner. The XO didn't even have a vehicle but, OK. While going through SRP (Soldier Readiness Processing) I was asked if I had seen a shrink in the last year. I answered honestly and said, "Yes." They decided to refer me to another shrink to clear me for deployment. When I let my new 1SG (First Sergeant) know what was going on, he lost his shit! He told me I was just trying to get out of deployment because I didn't like my duty position. He told me I was a piece of shit because, "Everybody has bad dreams! You just didn't answer the fucking questions right. But don't worry. We'll get you over to WTB (Warrior Transition Battalion) where they can get you out of the Army faster." I couldn't fucking believe this guy! Guys like him were the reason people didn't get help. Guys like 1SG Dickbag are the reason people try to push through it and end up suck-starting a shotgun. Fuck that guy and all of his ilk.

A few days after that encounter while loading MILVANS (shipping containers), I tried to catch a GP (General Purpose) medium tent from falling off a stack and tweaked my back. I figured I was fine, sucked down a few Motrin and called it good. That weekend while changing my daughter's diapers, I turned to grab the baby wipes and heard a pop and then couldn't move. The pain took my breath away. When I was able to finally move, I stood up and my wife said I was shaped like a question mark from the front. She took me to the ER and they did an MRI which revealed a ruptured disc, a herniated disc, a lateral shift (essentially a dislocated vertebrae) and some healed vertebral fractures. In short, my back was fucked. Shortly thereafter I was recommended for a med-board (MEB). And not for PTSD. Dick.

While going through the MEB process, the doctors went over everything that was ever wrong with me, which brought me back to seeing a psychologist on a regular basis. I sank into a really deep depression during that time. Between reliving some traumatic things in therapy and being MEBED, I was lost. Being a Soldier, in my eyes, was one of the only things that I ever did right in my life. I had made mistakes in every other aspect of my life, but I knew I could Soldier and it was being taken away from me. Between that and regaling my therapist with stories of car bombs and zipping up tiny body bags and remembering the smell of burnt flesh I was not in a good place. I actually contemplated suicide. I was a wreck. I couldn't provide anymore; I was only ever a Soldier and now I couldn't be that anymore. I figured I'd take a cocktail of Ativan and Vicodin and Insha'Allah. Try to do it before the SGLI (Service-members Group Life Insurance) was gone. The day before I planned on doing it I was sitting on the couch with my daughter and out of nowhere she looked up at me and said, "You're the best daddy ever! I love you!" I just responded with, "You're the best Maddy ever and I love you too!" At that moment, I realized I could never leave my family. I couldn't just quit like I had so many times before. The Army had taught me better than that. My kids and my wife were proud of what I had done and who I had become. I was proud of me for the first time in my life.

I've been (medically) retired from the Army for over five years now. I have a good job and a great relationship with my kids. My wife and I were touch and go for while primarily due to a lack of communicating our issues to each other. We are better now, though. I am better now. I see thing differently now. I know now that you have to talk about your problems. That applies to everything; not just nightmares and flashbacks. Talk to your spouse. Talk to your kids. If you don't, then you have no idea what's going on around you and you set yourself up for failure.

I have changed significantly from that dumb-ass kid in an apartment with my new wife. I don't quit when things get hard. I get through it. I don't keep things bottled up anymore. I don't yell...as much. The Army made me into someone I want to be.

The war changed me in different ways, too. Do I believe in God? Maybe I do and maybe I don't, but I definitely have a lot of questions. If he does exist, I'm not a big fan. I don't trust people. Large groups of people and the mob mentality that comes with them make me nervous. Tommy Lee Jones said, "A person is smart. People are dumb, panicky dangerous animals and you know it." I fully agree with that statement.

I'm more cynical and only try to take things at face value. I also understand the world is no longer black and white. There is huge gray area people fail to see.

I also believe that the only people that can help us (veterans) is us. No one else knows what we have done or seen. No one knows that smell like we do. No one understands the bond we have. There are people that I can't stand, but I know I can count on them when the bullets are going both ways. We have to stand up for each other. We have to talk to each other. We have to empower each other and let each other know that it's OK to be scared and that we can ask for help up when we fall down.

We are different. We run toward the sound of trouble. CSM Brian Shover told us once that no matter if someone served a month or 20 years you have to respect that because at least they tried to be better than themselves and you can't say that about 99% of the population.

And I'd do it all over again.

VIBRANIUM

Mat Vance

That Fresh-Faced Kid

After the phone lines in Virginia were finally restored after 9/11, I got a call from my Mom.

"I know what you and your friends are thinking, Mat. Don't do it. Please don't do it. At least finish school first."

I begrudgingly agreed to finish school even after speaking to a Marine recruiter and hoped there would still be a fight when I graduated. My generation had a fight and I was sitting in a classroom at Christopher Newport University. I was only a sophomore and time passed slowly as I tried to stay busy and sober long enough to pass each class. During winter break of my senior year, my Dad came into my room to wake me up on the night of Christmas Eve.

"Mat, can you help me carry your Mom into the car? I need to get her to the hospital."

I jumped out of bed and ran downstairs to get my Mom into the car. She had been fighting cancer for 9 years and sustained more pain and agony than anyone I've ever known. She never complained. Dad told me he would call when the doctors figured out how serious it was this time. Mom rolled down the window of the car as I looked at her from inside the garage thinking this might be it.

"I love you, Mom," I said with a quivering smile.
"I love you, Matty," she responded in the same manner.

It was the last time our eyes met as we spoke. She fought through Christmas day, passing away at 7am on December 26, 2003, with her loving husband and two kids

153

holding her. A friend of the family, Marine General George Flynn, who lost his Mom around the same age, told me the hard truth as I tried to grasp the emotions with, "It's a hole in your heart that will never be filled." I was in shock and just went back to school for my final semester where another friend, Meredith, who lost her father in an awful manner at a young age, saw me hiding behind a smile. She said, "It's going to hit you when you least expect it to." I got a call while sleeping one night in my apartment on campus during that last semester.

"Mat, it's going to be ok," my Mom said.

My Mom?! I ran down the hallway to tell my roommates my Mom was alive when I realized it was a dream. My heart sank for a moment, then I had a feeling of peace. I stopped caring so much about the little things and realized we have one life to live and we should live however the hell we want. I wanted to enlist! My Mom's wishes and school were the only reasons I wasn't in yet. I felt free to pursue a military life and did just that over spring break. I ended up choosing to go into the Army as a Cavalry Scout. Now I just wanted to get that damn degree and move on to something I really wanted.

School dragged and I drank furiously my last semester en route to a dismal performance for my senior thesis presentation. I tried to compare a person's musical preference to a fingerprint in the sense that everyone's choices are different for unknown reasons. I thought it was brilliant in my inebriated state of mind, but the professor gave me a D and I passed the course with a C. As I looked at the disappointing grade the professor smirkingly said, "At least you're graduating," as if I didn't even try and not knowing the loss my family just suffered. I wanted to punch her right in her witch-like nose. Alas, I did graduate on time and off I went into the military.

I didn't seek advice from my family on enlisting. I just did it and told them it was happening without a thought of what they were about to go through. It was definitely one of the most selfish things I have ever done. I was carefree and wanted to disappear from everyone and everything I knew in order to find myself. I wasn't thinking about how my Dad might not want the only person who could carry on the family name to go to war. I wasn't thinking about how my sister just lost a mother and I was the only person she could talk to that would understand her. Then there was the fact that war is dangerous and death is a good possibility so my family probably didn't want to go through another loss so soon after Mom. I was a straight-up asshole.

It wasn't until the days before my first deployment that I saw the toll it would take on my family. Neither my Dad nor my sister could look at me without tearing up as we said our "good-bye's" and they quickly walked away so I wouldn't see them cry. Then it sank in. Should I be doing this? What have I done to my family? What have I gotten myself into? Will I be a coward? Will I be able to lead my men? Will I be able to save everyone? If I die, I hope it's quick. Why am I getting butterflies in my stomach? Holy shit, stop thinking and be a leader. Do your job and protect your men at all costs. "Be steady in the face of death and if it's your time, then it's your time," was the Stonewall Jackson mentality I took into battle.

Before that deployment in 2006, my unit viewed PTS(D) as a term reserved for either mentally insane people that kill their cheating wives when they got home or for weak-minded soldiers that couldn't hack it. That was just the "Tough Guy" mentality at the time. We didn't want to make excuses for something that may impede our job performance, so we ignored what we couldn't understand. We didn't know a damn thing about the subject. We would soon be baptized by fire and that fact was only a fraction of what we would experience.

"It's a good day to die! Ha-ha-ha!"

After training in the cold rains of the Pacific Northwest, I headed to the dry desert terrain of Iraq in 118 degrees. This place was death. An unforgiving environment that brought sweat soaking through my boots to the ground where it dried instantly. When I finally dried off, my uniform crunched with my own body salt crumbling off. The smell. I will never forget the smell. It was the smell of human beings taking on the carnal actions of animals. We saw dead bodies on a very consistent basis lying around... just because. "The Surge" was complete madness. If insurgents, militia or terrorists weren't attacking us, they were attacking each other. They captured for ransom, or tortured and killed all because of a different sect of the same religion. Iraqi people that lost family or had to kill simply used, "Insha'Allah," (If Allah wills it) as the excuse or reasoning. We experienced ambushes, IED's, RPG's, grenades, complex ambushes and getting caught in the crossfire of sectarian violence as we had to shoot at both sides. We had to make split second decisions that could ruin lives if we chose wrong. Bullets snapped all around us. How were we alive after being so close to death so many times? Only afterwards could we wonder. During the melee, we were psychologically immune to the danger, only looking out for each other.

There's not just one moment that I think about. When I think back to both of my deployments, I remember many things as there are so many events. Some things make me sad, some make me angry and some make me laugh my ass off. Mostly I think of events where human nature burned so bright, whether good or evil.

The things my platoon and I have seen...

We've seen each other kill. We've saved each other's lives. We've saved thousands of civilian lives. We've given aid to the wounded. We've seen the insides of mutilated bodies and bodies that met our wrath or the enemy's wrath. We've seen what losing a best friend in the worst way does to a man. We've seen what being taken off the battlefield, away from your brothers, to be medically treated does to a man. We've seen best friends attack each other. We've seen atrocities on all sides. We've seen men start shooting at little kids playing soccer, hitting two of them for no reason. We've seen a man shoot an old man in the back because he picked up a weapon at 200 yards after a firefight was clearly over then snicker at his son who watched it happen. We've seen men break. We've seen men try to kill themselves because of an unfaithful woman. We've seen men shoot themselves to get sent home. We've seen locals go crazy and start slapping themselves while their insurgent family member bleeds out. We've done house raids to capture evil men. We've gone 48 hours with no sleep. We've seen bravery and courage not get recognized. We've seen betrayal and cowardice go unpunished. We've seen these things and so much more.

When I do think about these events in my life, I don't see them as having a negative impact on me. I'm certainly a better person because of them. I found myself on the battle field. Before war, I was a daydreamer looking for an opportunity to become a leader and when I rose to the occasion with my brothers, I never looked back. Before every mission, I would take a moment to myself, put my hand over my heart, bow my head, close my eyes and whisper to myself,

"God, help my men today. Help me be strong to protect them. If anyone should fall, let it be me. Thank you."

And, it's tattooed on my ribcage now. It's not that I wanted to die, but I couldn't fathom seeing any of my brothers killed. Seeing one of them wounded was one of the two things that caused me to breakdown. I would go visit, see their wounds and their pain, crack a joke to make them smile and quickly leave because my eyes started to swell with tears. It's for those reasons that many of us are completely fine putting ourselves in the worst positions and dealing with the cards we're dealt all in the name of protecting our own.

The other time I broke down overseas is when my friend Meredith's words came true. We had just finished a stressful night mission and were hanging out at our Strykers (vehicles). We were smoking cigarettes, venting and making each other laugh. At some point in the conversation someone cracked a joke and we all started to laugh uncontrollably and it just started a rapid chain reaction of memories that led back to Mom. As the guys kept laughing louder and louder, I got quiet and couldn't control the emotions so I turned to walk between two Strykers.

"Vance! Where you going?" one soldier asked.
"I just gotta take a piss man! Wanna watch or somethin'?"
"Fuck you! You'd be so lucky!" more laughter faded as everything came crashing down.

I got to the far end of the Stryker, turned the corner and

just let loose. My body started to bend over, my knees buckled as my hands covered my face. I hadn't cried like that since I was a kid. The stress of war had built up so much that my emotions were just waiting for something to break the dam holding them back and it ended up being a reaction to a memory of my Mom. I missed her so much. It definitely hit me when I least expected it: 3 years after she had passed away and I was a battle-hardened veteran. I had to quickly recover so the guys wouldn't see me so broken. I ended up coming back to sit on top of a Stryker by myself later that night to reflect. The horizon lit up with tracer fire looking like comets and explosions making flashes of light with the mushroom cloud rising above the concrete jungle. What a life. What an adventure I was on. PTS(D) still wasn't even a thought in my mind. I just wanted to be a great soldier.

Beyond the Rage

Originally, I wanted to be a lifer, or career military. There were so many opportunities the military had to offer. It was between deployments that I noticed a major shift in how things were being conducted in the military. People started talking about their feelings more and the hard men that brought me up as a puppy had disappeared. Leaders were soft and only looking out for themselves. The dirt bags were getting promoted for sticking around long enough and hopping onto the "good-ole boys" bandwagon. Fewer men were standing up to simply do the right thing. Weaklings had a fear of losing favor with the soft men's asses they were kissing, so they seldom took action. This was not what I wanted with my life. The opportunities were still there, but I wasn't having fun anymore. I didn't get excited to go to work. I became anxious because I didn't trust the people I was serving under.

I decided I would get out after my second deployment and that deployment would be the longest year of my life. Clicks formed. Leaders chose favorites and shunned non-favorites in a world where fraternizing wasn't even supposed to be allowed. A black superior looked me right in the face and said, "I hate white people," and forbid me from disciplining his black subordinate friend. A lieutenant refused to heed my tactical advice, because he personally didn't like me. He then did his own thing and men were wounded. I stuck by his side even when I knew something bad was going to happen. I, and many others, almost died because of his many poor decisions. We never got a thank you. What in the fuck was happening to my Army?

I pleaded with my men, who were on their first deployment, to hang in there. If they could make it through this year of their lives, they could make it through anything. It wasn't like my first deployment where we had some form of enemy contact every day. It was more like once a month. That opened the doors for complacency. It was towards the end of the deployment where men were wounded and killed. The enemy watched us tear each other apart, watched our movements, our style and struck when we were thinking of being home so soon. I couldn't wait to get home and be done with this group of "leaders" and move on with my life.

As we came home and went our separate ways during leave, I had time to think. I went back to out-process after leave and I saw different faces on the men that had done shameful things. It was as if they knew they were wrong, but too proud to admit it. I turned my attention to the younger soldiers. They deserved better leaders and adventures than what they got. I was excited to see them in action, but seldom had that opportunity. They performed well when those moments did come. They were about to go to different units and I wanted to make sure they would succeed so I gave them as much help as I could. It was then that a lot of people really brought PTS(D) to my attention.

It was something we all became aware of in time, but studies were and still are in their early stages. We knew PTS(D) was now a part of us. We knew it was a natural reaction to what we experienced and not actually a sign of being crazy or weak-minded. Because of my experiences, I am more alert, but not on a paranoid level. I'm aware of everything around me when I walk into a room, but I don't avoid windows or constantly have my back to a wall. I sweat in large crowds, but that's not because of war; it's because I've never liked big crowds. I'm more irritable, but that's because I sense weakness and poor decision making, not because of wild, black and white flashbacks. I have dreams and thoughts of intense moments, but it's only to point out the mistakes I made so I never repeat them.

Books and movies with embellished stories have seemingly given people a way to act and it's wrong. Some men do go through those stereotypical moments and they are sincere, but in talking with my men and the veterans they have encountered, I have noticed many veterans want the attention and think they have to act a certain way. Everyone wants to know someone that was killed. That's fucking horrible and I'm thankful every day of my life that the ones closest to me made it out alive. The ones that embellish don't realize the very thing that makes them stronger people is being used as an excuse to not be... their service. Be proud that you served, whether it be at a desk or on the front lines. You volunteered to take that oath. Because of you, there was no draft. Be proud.

I've been in close proximity to several IED's and shot at. I've been knocked out. I have ringing in my ears. It usually doesn't last long. Sometimes it's faint and other times it's deafening. All of my joints are stiff. My neck cracks every time I move my head. My jaw is always tight and also cracks. I developed a stutter that I had to work on to fix. I have to slow down my speech or people will pick up on it. I have this strange brain-to-mouth disconnect where I can see a word in my head, but it comes out as something completely different. I don't even know what the hell that is. I don't complain about all that to people, because every time something cracks it reminds me of what I did... and I smile.

The notion of being spaced out because I'm having sweaty flashbacks is erroneous. It's not a thousand-yard stare for me. I space out and stare into the distance sometimes because I'm thinking of the most exciting time in my life. I'm back there thinking of the action and how I miss the adrenaline. I miss being depended on and asked to do scary, risky things that made my heart pound and men looked to me to lead them without hesitation. I miss being at my best. I miss the close calls as we pushed forward. I miss grinning at my men as they showed fear... then they smiled with me and that turned to a crazy laugh because they believed in me as much as I believed in them to get the job done and get the job done right.

Have I been affected by war? Certainly. Have I had the most horrific experiences? Not even close. There are both physical and psychological differences in me. I experienced tragedy before the military with several family members and a friend passing away, two in my arms. Some men enter the military without having lost a pet. Those men will handle war differently than me. Then, I look at each man. Some feel entitled. Some feel like they need to one-up those around them. Some stay quiet. Some kill themselves. Some cry. Some compensate for a lack of combat action with falsehoods. I believe in being a quiet professional; to push forward with what you've learned and taking advantage of those lessons to better yourself without running your mouth about it. Who is right and who is wrong? I don't think there's an answer. We're talking about something we can't entirely grasp yet. All I can say is that from what I've seen and what goes through my head on a daily basis, PTS(D) is different in every human being. It's like that damn fingerprint thesis of mine back in college. No two people will handle it the same way and who the hell knows why people do what they do. I only hope those who are having a hard time reach out to the ones that were there, because nobody else will come close to understanding.

I get that PTS(D) is a natural reaction to something you're not used to experiencing. So, what does it mean when you're diagnosed, then you go back to war, then come home and miss the very thing you're not supposed to be used to? Has it been reversed? Do I need to constantly be at war to feel normal? I'm happy to be home and at peace in the United States, but I still miss so much of war. I think there is a step missing in the process of diagnosis. The term PTS(D) itself is very broad and can be abused by embellishing crybabies when people with legitimate issues are unfortunately thrown into the same category. It is my belief that we need to look at this subject matter in a whole new way, from scratch, and together.

THE BATTLE WITHIN

Phillip Trezza

> Time is never time at all.
> You can never ever leave without leaving a piece of youth.
> And our lives are forever changed.
> We will never be the same.
> The more you change the less you feel.
> -Billy Corgan

The memories I've collected have ultimately shaped who I am, the way I think, and my outlook on life. This collection of memories has been crudely crafted and haphazardly pieced together by events that were good enough, bad enough, scary enough, intense enough, funny enough, or overall significant enough to chisel a small nook into my mind and plant itself there for the rest of eternity.

I have come to the belief that occasionally we are forced to barter with these lasting memories and the events that create them. It seems that when a particular event occurs, one of sufficient significance, we take a piece of that event with us in the form of a memory. We often create the memory from an event because the event changes the prior perception that we had of the world. At the same time, we collect this memory and new perception, we are often forced to leave a piece of ourselves behind. The piece of ourselves that we are forced to relinquish is our previous, and now outdated, perception of the world.

Events that transpire during conflict are significant and create unique and vivid memories. A Soldier ends up collecting many pieces of these events during a journey through combat. And, with each sad or disturbing memory collected, a piece of the Soldier's innocence, faith in humanity, faith in one's self and the positive perception of the world are slowly sacrificed.

With each lifeless body, each dead child, with each wet grasp of bloody and slippery skin, with each moan and gasp for breath, with each cry, scream and shriek of women speaking in an unfamiliar language, with every explosion, with every sprint down a dark and dangerous highway toward the wounded, with each injured, bleeding or unconscious friend, with every letter from home, and with each time I helped to put a dead person into a large black bag, I gained a memory and lost a small piece of myself. I lost a little bit of the person I used to be.

There are several ways one's body and mind attempt to both react and acclimate to repeated traumatic stimuli; the type of stimuli a Service Member or, in my case, an Army Medic is subjected to. There are also several ways that a person can attempt to cope with repeated traumatic experiences. I believe that this unconscious attempt by the body and mind to acclimate, as well as the conscious efforts of the individual to cope with the emotions produced by repeated traumatic stimuli, are instrumental to the development and severity of Post-Traumatic Stress Disorder.

Combat Medics are not given many options in regard to how to cope with repetitive traumatic experiences during a combat deployment. This is because the Medic, especially one that is in a platoon full of Cavalry Scouts and Infantrymen, is expected to never be bothered by the horrors of war. After all, it is the Medic's job to perform tasks like tying tourniquets onto snapped and severed limbs, or trying to triage and treat an overwhelming amount of patients after a car bomb explosion on a busy street corner in Baghdad. The Medic really only has one way of dealing with these ongoing traumatic experiences and that is to train the mind and the emotions to *feel* less. The Medic can be successful if he or she is able to suppress or desensitize the emotions that come naturally with seeing horrible and disturbing things.

Though I was able to regulate how I dealt with my emotions during my time overseas sufficiently enough to perform my duties well, it has taken me several years to adjust the way I perceive the world around me to a more "normal" perspective. I was also left with several questions: Was it healthy for me to continue in this line of work if it meant that I would have to commit to abandoning emotion? Because, that would certainly be the only way in which I would be able to continue to perform Combat Medic duties at a high level. What happens when a person suppresses so much of what they feel for an extended period of time? Do other Medics feel the same ways that I do?

I have received answers to these questions much too often over the last decade. I am frequently contacted by Medics that I went to Medic school with about friends from our graduating class and their untimely deaths. Some are due to combat, but many more have occurred when they get home from deployment or after they get out of the Army completely. Many of these brave men end up self-medicating themselves to death. Some take their own lives. Others have been killed in altercations stemming from an inability to control their actions and emotions. One friend in particular was killed by police when he tried to pull a weapon on them at the end of a high-speed pursuit. These deaths are the product of human minds attempting to cope with repeated traumatic experiences and not being able to do so adequately. These deaths happen when people suppress the emotions they *should* feel for much too long.

To feel no emotion can make for a miserable existence. It is unnatural. It can also lead an individual to make dangerous choices. Conversely, to be overcome with a collection of traumatic experience can slowly eat away at a person's soul. The struggle to stay between these two ends of the emotional spectrum is ultimately the plight of the Combat Medic and all Combat Soldiers.

This battle within is the unseen and unheard enemy that is present in every conflict, and that follows each Warrior if they are lucky enough to make it home.

FORGED BY FIRE

"Crazy Horse 6"

Who was I before the military?

Before joining the Army, I was a regular kid from Florida who enjoyed playing sports, hanging out with friends, and having fun. I always took academic achievement very seriously, but I did not really stress out much because I learned to be a good test taker, and many of the subjects came easily for me. I never really planned to join the Army and after high school I was going to join a majority of my friends and go to college at the University of Florida. Midway through my junior year of high school my cousin invited me to visit him at West Point and see what the United States Military Academy was all about. He was a senior preparing to graduate and be commissioned as an officer in the Army. I had a great visit and decided to apply for admission. A few months later, I received my acceptance letter to join the West Point Class of 2000. I shipped off for Cadet Basic Training a few weeks after high school graduation. Unlike some of my classmates, I had no idea what to expect and had not really considered a career in the Army. Much like high school, I quickly figured out how to excel academically and before I knew it I was graduating and commissioning as a Second Lieutenant in the Armor Branch. I was joining the Army during a time of relative peace. Regional conflicts in Bosnia and Kosovo were the hotspots at the time and few people discussed terrorism, conflict in the Middle East, or the possibility of fighting in a large-scale conflict.

After graduation, I went to Fort Knox for Officer Basic Training to learn mounted maneuver warfare and the employment of M1-A1 Abrams Main Battle Tanks. Before reporting to my first duty station after the Officer Basic Course, I married my longtime girlfriend who was now an officer in the United States Coast Guard. After getting married and spending time on our honeymoon, my first assignment was at Fort Lewis, Washington, as a Mobile Gun System Platoon Leader in Charlie Company, 2nd Battalion, 3rd Infantry Regiment, as part of the newly created 3rd Stryker Bridge Combat Team, 2nd Infantry Division. The Stryker Brigade was in its infancy and my platoon used an Italian made wheeled vehicle known as a Centauro to train for combat while the Stryker vehicle was being developed. Life in the early days of the Stryker Brigade were interesting as an Armor Officer in an Infantry company. Our platoon was routinely used in an opposing force role to battle against the Infantry line platoons. I quickly learned the ways of dismounted patrolling, Infantry battle drills, and a host of other light infantry skills and tactics that were not routinely trained by Armor units, but would be crucial later in my career as a Cavalry officer. Within a few months of joining Charlie Company, I watched on live TV as the second plane hit the World Trade Center on September 11, 2001. We had no idea what was happening, but we knew that our lives would never be the same.

Who was I during war?

About two years after the 9-11 terrorist attacks, the newly formed 3/2 Stryker Bridge Combat Team deployed to Iraq and road-marched from Kuwait to Samarra, Iraq, to support the 4th Infantry Division for about a month at FOB Pacesetter. Shortly after arriving, our brigade experienced the first casualties of the deployment when a Stryker rolled into a canal and several Soldiers drowned. Our Squadron's first significant contact was a rocket attack that impacted near our tents. In the early days of the war, we were living in tents with very little protection from indirect fire, so this first attack was jarring. It was nighttime and pitch dark and while running for cover I fell into a deep ditch, which was hilarious after the rocket attack ended, and I crawled out of the ditch without injury. After a month of operating in Samarra, our brigade conducted a Relief in Place with elements of the 101st Airborne Division (Air Assault) in Mosul and Tal Afar. After a month of living in tents, not showering and sharing one Porta Potty for the entire Squadron, it was nice to move to FOB Fulda with living containers, showers, flushing toilets, and an excellent dining facility. We were told that the Mosul area had been tamed and was a relatively nice place to be. Violence was down and the Iraqi people had begun to rebuild their lives.

During the deployment, I was the Squadron Assistant S-4 (Logistics) and later the Squadron S-4 for 1st Squadron, 14th Cavalry Regiment. After spending nearly two years training for war as a platoon leader in both an Infantry Company and later in a Stryker Reconnaissance Squadron, the transition to "life on staff" and the different mission set was significant. I quickly became close friends with my fellow staff officers and we found meaningful ways to contribute to the success of the Squadron. Regardless of our duty titles, we routinely volunteered to join logistic resupply missions or any other mission with Headquarters Troop to get us "outside the wire" and into the fight. The first IED strike that occurred on our Squadron in Tal Afar hit a resupply convoy that I and a few of my staff buddies were part of. The first Purple Heart of the deployment went to my good friend who was in the vehicle in front of me. It occurred on a moonless night, very close to our FOB, and the bright blast and thunderous sound was disorienting. I was driving the HMMWV (High Mobility Multipurpose Wheeled Vehicle) because our regular driver was on leave. I experienced a strange, almost out of body, experience driving the HMMWV while hyper-focused on the road ahead of me and oblivious to the sights, sounds, and smells around me. Somehow, I drove the HMMWV through the middle of a traffic circle, through several barricades, concertina wire, and a guardrail, and then rejoined the middle of the convoy that was on the far side of the traffic circle. We quickly realized that things were a bit more dangerous than we had first assumed. The honeymoon phase had ended.

The remainder of the year-long deployment had its ups and downs with several close calls from IED strikes and indirect fire along the way. Although never physically wounded, I had a few near misses including an IED strike in front of my HMMWV (with no windows or doors) that left me with ringing in my ears for several hours, several ambushes on convoys I was on, and sporadic indirect fire attacks on the FOB. Tragedy struck one night when a Legal Clerk who worked on staff with me was killed in an IED strike that also wounded my good friend. The Legal Clerk volunteered to be a machine gunner during a routine logistics patrol. He was killed less than a mile away from the FOB in an area that we routinely traveled. His death was the first for the Squadron and marked the first time during the deployment that I felt a tremendous sense of sadness and loss. Fortunately, I had several very close friends on staff to decompress from the situation and we quickly adjusted to the new norm of having a good friend and a member of our staff killed in action. After the deployment ended we headed home to reintegrate with our families and prepare for the next deployment.

Less than two years after returning from Iraq, we were headed back for another year in Iraq. The two years home passed very quickly with training exercises, ranges, and a rotation to the National Training Center. I was now the Troop Commander, responsible for the lives of 105 Soldiers, 17 Stryker vehicles, and millions of dollars of equipment. It was a significant responsibility and I was unsure of my ability to handle the challenge of command, especially in an increasingly hostile environment. We deployed in June 2006 and the insurgency in Iraq was in full swing. Iraq was on the brink of a civil war and the news coming from Iraq seemed to get worse each day. Our Brigade was thrust into the heart of Baghdad during the start of the Surge to help turn the tide in the battle for Iraq. The main differences between deploying as a member of staff in 2003-04 and now as the Troop Commander in 2006 were the tremendous increase in level of responsibility, the heightened level of personal risk and experiencing a significant amount of social isolation that supported the adage that "command is lonely." Unlike staff where you have several officer peers that you work with daily, as the Troop Commander everyone you routinely interact with is one of your subordinates. Although you love them like family and would do anything for them, you cannot speak freely to your men about your thoughts, emotions, uncertainties, and feelings about the war. You can certainly confide in senior NCOs (Non-Commissioned Officers) and officers about some issues, but they are not your friends and cannot be your peers. The Squadron Task Force lived together on the FOB, so I was able to routinely interact with other Commanders and staff officers of the Squadron. Much like the first deployment, having a supportive network of friends was crucial to my emotional well-being. My wife and I routinely spoke via email and the occasional phone call, but there are things that you do not want to burden your spouse with, especially some of the horrible realties of war, the close calls, the fear, and responsibilities of command. I was fortunate to become close friends with our Squadron Chaplain and he changed my life in several meaningful ways that I will discuss later.

Our Troop and Squadron experienced a great deal of success during our 15-month deployment to Iraq. We spent most of our time operating south of Baghdad in the Abu Dishir/Al Doura neighborhoods and later in the heart of Baghdad on Haifa Street. Partnering with and building the capacity and legitimacy of the Iraqi Army and National Police were both major objectives to help transition the responsibility for security to the host nation forces. Our area of operations in Abu Dishir was on an ethnic fault-line between Sunni and Shia neighborhoods and Iraqi-on-Iraqi violence was more common than Iraqi-on-US Army violence. Oftentimes our patrols would move to the sound of the guns and arrive shortly after a territorial fight between Sunni and Shia that often left civilian casualties dying in the streets. "Extra-judicial killings" and targeted torture and murder of Iraqi civilians was commonplace by both groups. Some days our patrols would come upon several dead bodies, often mutilated in horrible ways. Both sides were quick to blame each other and our unit was often caught in-between, with no way to know who was at fault for the violence. We did our best to reduce violence, restore essential services, and capture/kill insurgent forces, while also building the capacity of the Iraqi Security Forces. We captured several large caches and detained several Brigade-level "High Value Targets" in our area of operations.

By far, the most intense combat our Troop experienced occurred during an out-of-sector mission to Diwayniah in southern Iraq. Our Squadron conducted a deliberate attack into the heart of a Shia stronghold in order to disrupt enemy operations and restore control of the area to US and Coalition Forces. Oud Troop entered the city as the sun was rising and we saw Iraqi Security Forces leaving town with white flags displayed. Although it was now daylight, there was virtually no one outside, police checkpoints were abandoned. We knew that we were heading into a fight. After about 12 hours of intense fighting, which included multiple IED attacks, RPG, direct fire attacks, and indirect fire attacks, the level of violence decreased significantly. After 36 hours of straight combat operations outside the wire, I was physically exhausted and in desperate need of sleep. Over the next few days, we continued to exploit our initial successes and, in the end, our Troop and Squadron won a decisive victory with numerous enemy captured and killed, several weapons and munitions caches seized, and no significant friendly casualties or damage to equipment. I was very proud of how well the Troop performed in the longest duration of intense combat we had experienced during the deployment. After months of minor successes and minor set-backs, it felt great to clearly win in a decisive engagement with a determined and relatively well-organized enemy.

After relocating to the heart of Baghdad for operations along the infamous Haifa Street, we spent the remainder of our deployment building the capacity of our Combat Outpost, and training and supporting our partners in the Iraqi Security Forces. We did a lot of combined operations with the Iraqis and we saw some improvement in their ability to conduct security and counter-insurgency operations. Our time at Haifa Street was relatively uneventful despite the reputation for violence in the area. Since we were nearing the end of an extended deployment, I was concerned that Soldiers on patrol would become complacent and lapses in security would result in casualties. The Squadron's only casualty during our time there occurred when a Soldier failed to properly ground a fueler before refueling a running generator. A large fire ensued that severely burned the Soldier who later died of her injuries. Fortunately, because of the heroic actions of our Troop Executive Officer the flaming fueler was moved away from the barracks and there were no further casualties. The death of a Soldier to an avoidable accident was a stark reminder of the high price of complacency in combat. I prayed there would be no more injury or death so close to the end of our tour.

As the 15-month deployment came to an end, I was very proud of all that our Troop had accomplished in Iraq. We had done a lot of good through a broad spectrum of operations ranging from intense combat to providing aid to Iraqis in need.

We helped rebuild schools, restore essential services, reduce levels of violence, and help Iraqis return to a more normal life than they had experienced in the last 15 months. Our Troop had achieved significant success and our Troop only suffered one major casualty during a grenade attack that required a Soldier to be evacuated from Iraq. I was extraordinarily proud and relieved to bring all my Soldiers home alive and well. As we returned home from 15 months of war during a critical time in Operation Iraqi Freedom, I knew that we left Iraq a better place than it was when we arrived and I was able to bring all my Soldiers home to their families. The tremendous burden of personal responsibility and constant stress was lifted the minute all members of my command returned home. To this day and likely for the rest of my career, bringing all my Soldiers home alive from 15 months of combat remains my greatest professional accomplishment. I remain connected with a majority of my Soldiers and I enjoy hearing about their triumphs and successes as they grow. Many have separated from the Army, but some are still in uniform and doing great things!

Who am I now, still serving?

After deploying for 27 months in a span of four years and completing a 30-month troop command tour, I wanted a change of pace so I could focus on my family. My wife and I had been married for six years, but had only spent one anniversary together and missed numerous birthdays, Thanksgivings, Christmases, and other holidays. We did not have children yet and we wanted to start a family. While deployed, I was selected to attend graduate school for two years with a follow-on teaching assignment at West Point. During this time, I opted into the Human Resource Manager Career Field. A year later, this career field merged with the Adjutant General Branch and suddenly I went from being an Armor Officer to being an Adjutant General Officer. This was an unexpected and sudden transition from being a combat arms officer who commanded a Cavalry Troop in combat to being a human resource professional who was now destined to be a career staff officer.

Part of my personal and professional identity was as a

combat arms leader who had served on the tip of the spear in combat for most of my young career. I now had to readjust my self-concept to include my new role as a Force Sustainment leader who would contribute to the mission through superior staff work and collaboration. Fortunately, I had time to assimilate to this new mindset during a three-year teaching tour at West Point. Afterward, I commanded once again, but this time as a commander of a Military Entrance Processing Station (MEPS). Commanding a MEPS was a complete 180 degree turn from commanding a Cavalry Troop. Leading Soldiers who had initiative, innovation, and discipline had been replaced by managing a mostly civilian staff who excelled in mediocrity, drama, and working just hard enough not to be fired. For the first time in my professional career, I was not excited to go to work each day. My motivation and morale were sapped almost daily by a few employees who were petty, lazy, and obstacles to progress and innovation. A random selection of 20 Soldiers from my old Cavalry Troop could have completed the mission at the MEPS to a higher standard, in less time, with half the staff and with 100% less drama. The two-year command tour at the MEPS was the most challenging of my career and the least rewarding. The mission to screen and process the young men and women who volunteered to serve in the military was incredible, but managing the people who executed this important mission made it challenging and a soul-sucking experience. This tour, once again, reinforced the saying that "command is lonely," but this time I didn't have peers on staff or in adjacent units to commiserate with. Fortunately, during the last year of my command I was blessed with the addition of an outstanding senior enlisted advisor who became by my trusted agent and friend. Without him, the last year would have likely driven me crazy.

Today, I continue to serve as a member of the Army Staff and I am committed to serving both in and out of uniform for the rest of my life. Throughout my career, I have been blessed to be surrounded by great Soldiers, NCOs, and officers and have had the rare good fortune never to have had a bad boss. I was set-up for success in every job I had and was selected for promotion and command ahead of my peers on several occasions. My success was not my own but rather the result of the collective efforts of those I've had the privilege to serve with and for. I was honored to be promoted to the rank of Lieutenant Colonel and given the opportunity to serve in the Army until retirement.

My interpretation of the world now vs. the world I knew before war.

My experiences during combat fundamentally shaped who I was for the better. These experiences molded the remainder of my life and enabled me to be a better husband, father, officer and person, in general. Before deploying, I took so much for granted and only saw the world through the eyes of a citizen of the most powerful and prosperous country in the history of the world. The United States has its faults and not all share in the abundance of resources, goodwill, and freedom, but collectively we experience a standard of living far beyond what most people in foreign countries can even imagine. Our system of government is stable, our laws promote individual rights and liberties, and in general our citizens can live in peace without fear of attack. Living in Iraq for 27 months made me gain a new appreciation for life, beauty, family, and the amazing fortune of being born a U.S. citizen. After witnessing abject poverty, humanitarian crisis, sectarian violence, government corruption, and seeing people live in fear of their neighbors, their police and military, and their government, it was hard not to regain a new appreciation for the good fortune of living in the United States.

Upon returning to the United States and resuming a normal life I became acutely aware of how blessed I was. Unlike some combat Veterans who become cynical and angry at the sense of entitlement of the majority of Americans who have never served, I instead felt happy to live in a country that provided so much individual freedom and security. Instead of living in constant fear and unable to effect change, citizens of the U.S. are able to do as they wish without fear of government reprisal, attack by citizens of a different ethnic or religious group, or control by foreign powers. I've always been an optimist, but after returning from two tours in Iraq, I've become a raging optimist who believes that the best is yet to come. The opportunities for success and prosperity in the United States are without peer anywhere else in the world and, although not perfect, our potential for success is limited not by the government or foreign powers, but by ourselves.

How the war changed my family and I.

Prior to deploying I was a mediocre husband and son. I took for granted the love I experienced from my family and my wife. I spoke to my parents a few times a month and visited when I could, but it seemed routine and I didn't go out of my way to tell my parents how much I loved them or how much I appreciated all that they had done for me. My wife and I had a good relationship, but had spent more time apart then we had been together during our first six years of marriage. Being separated and isolated from family created a sense of longing, bonding, and appreciation that I had previously not experienced. After missing numerous holidays, birthdays, weddings, and family gatherings because of deployment, I now realized how meaningful family was and how strongly I desired to be closer to them. After 27 months of war, I became more in love with my wife and gained greater appreciation for her. She had stayed by my side and supported me through training, deployments, and extended periods of separation. I now express my love more frequently to both my family and my wife and I've gained a much closer relationship with my sister. Being gone for so long and in such trying conditions enabled me to realize how blessed I am and how much I had taken for granted.

Another positive result of war was growing closer to God and a strengthening of my faith. Growing up I had always gone to church and considered myself a Christian, but I had gone through the motions and convinced myself I was secure in my faith, but my actions were not always consistent. Prior to the second deployment I had attended church sporadically, I prayed occasionally, I rarely tithed or contributed to charity, and I frequently used foul language at work and sometimes at home. I was an apathetic Christian and I did not have a close relationship with God. During my time in command, I was blessed to become friends with the Squadron Chaplain who renewed my faith and helped re-establish my personal relationship with God. He challenged me spiritually in ways I had never been challenged before, and I routinely attended church services while deployed even though it cut into precious sleep time. I made it a personal mission to read the entire Bible during the deployment and after one memorable time of being called out by the Chaplain for using foul language, I made a personal commitment to stop speaking in such a manner. To this day, I avoid using foul language and try to set a positive example for others.

I truly believed that the Squadron Chaplain saved my faith and got me back on track with my relationship with God. This relationship with God has made me a better husband and a better father. I am more charitable, more loving, and have a renewed sense of appreciation and wonder with the grace that Jesus provides. I believe in miracles and I personally experienced the grace of God while deployed. While on a routine search operation with Iraqi forces I was standing behind a chest-high courtyard wall outside a home that was being searched. I was talking with my Fire Support Officer when a hail of machine gun fire impacted all around us, striking the wall in front of us and the house behind us. In a "Pulp Fiction"-like moment I looked up and realized how many bullet holes where in the house right where I had been standing. There is no rational explanation for how all the bullets missed me and my Fire Support Officer (also a devout Christian) except for God's grace in the form of a miracle. I believe that God saved my life in Iraq so that I could inspire others to be better people, to live a better life, and to contribute to the greater good. I don't feel called to convert others to my faith, but rather live my life in a way that inspires other people to be good people. Without experiencing God's grace first-hand, my faith in God and His divine presence would probably not be the same.

My interpretation of PTSD/PTS,
Post-traumatic stress (PTS) is a real challenge for some combat Veterans, but people need to understand that it can and does happen to people whether they have served in the military or not. Too many Soldiers put additional pressures on themselves to "be normal," because they feel that something is wrong with them when they are experiencing PTS. PTS is a completely normal response to an abnormal situation.

Whether experiencing acute trauma in war or while in a car accident in the States, PTS can occur as the human body tries to cope with a life or death situation. I am by no means an expert on PTS or any other behavioral health challenges, but I do know that PTS does not make someone "broken" or "abnormal" and it can happen to anyone. Two people may experience the exact same event but they process it in different ways. One person may not experience PTS and the other might, but it does not mean that one person is stronger than the other or that the person who seeks assistance for PTS is weak in any way. True strength is admitting that you need help and then seeking it. The military has worked hard to combat stigma associated with seeking help, but until Soldiers feel free to share their experiences with others, then people will continue to hide their private battles and invisible wounds of war in order to appear strong.

Although I have not personally experienced any symptoms of PTS, I have experienced a closely-related phenomenon, which is probably as common: post-traumatic growth. I truly believe that after experiencing war - the unexpected attacks, death and injury of close friends and fellow Soldiers, the killing of combatants, civilian casualties, fear, uncertainty, and a constant state of low-level stress – everyone is changed in some way. Research shows that some people actually experience positive growth after a traumatic event and these experiences shape their lives for the better. I have no idea how I grew from the same experiences that caused others to experience PTS, but I do not think that I am stronger than those who have struggled. I know many hard-charging resilient officers, NCOs and Soldiers who have had symptoms of PTS during and after deployments. Fortunately, many of these individuals found positive ways to cope with PTS and reached out to others for help. I would like to believe I would have done the same thing if in their situation, but you never know what you would actually do until you are in the same situation.

I think many combat Veterans, if they thought about it, would realize that they have been changed in positive ways as a result of being in combat. Although the media and our society likes to publicize the bad news stories, the tragedies, and the "broken Veteran narrative," I believe that many Veterans have positive side effects of war as well. Each Soldier in combat has a tremendous amount of responsibility and accountability placed squarely on their shoulders each day and their actions have life or death consequences. Young men and women in combat are thrust into roles and levels of responsibility that their civilian peers will likely never experience in their lifetime. These experiences in combat grow mission-focused, disciplined, and adaptive leaders who are comfortable being uncomfortable and who can thrive in the face of adversity.

Much like steel is harden in fire, Veterans are forged in the furnace of combat. Veterans are not broken by combat, rather they are tested, hardened, and strengthened in ways that can only come about from being put in such extreme situations. There are limits to this growth and even the hardest steel will melt if the fire is too hot for too long. Therefore, leaders must be careful to mitigate risks, not expose Soldiers to unnecessary danger, and set an ethical leadership climate. Combat Veterans, regardless if they have experienced PTS or post-traumatic growth, are civic assets who have the ability to shape national policy, effect positive change, and lead in both the private and public sector. The "broken Veteran" narrative is damaging for both the Nation and the warfighters who protect it. Instead of seeing combat Veterans as charity cases who need to be taken care of, we should focus our attention on the tremendous amount of good that combat Veterans do. The best way we can support our Nation's warriors is not by pitying them, but rather by leveraging them in continued service to the Nation. Combat Veterans need equal opportunity for success, not handouts or sympathy. Combat Veterans must hold ourselves to a higher standard and find ways to continue to serve and lead at home and in our communities. The experiences down range have shaped and molded us into the people we are today and we must find ways to see the good that shines through and share that goodness with others.

RIPPED OPEN

Joshua D. LeBel

WHERE PTSD LIVED WITH ME
It happened so quickly, without any notice, and changed everything in an instant.

"The body exploded, it just exploded," I said after I had crawled along a floor and out of a room I was just searching.

My Soldiers and I were conducting a search of a building that held some recently dead Afghan fighters. During the engagement, we were able to kill all the fighters and now had to search the bodies for anything that could help us in the future. One of the bodies needed to be turned over to conduct a search of the body. All of those things you hear about happening when you experience a near death experience - life flashing before your eyes and whatever - it's a bunch of shit. The only thing I thought of right away was how bad everything hurt and how much I needed to get out of that room and back to the rest of the Soldiers.

My name is Sergeant First Class (SFC) Joshua LeBel and on January 12, 2012, about half way through a year-long deployment in Afghanistan, my life took a turn that still affects me to this day. Understanding Post Traumatic Stress Disorder (PTSD) is something that can be hard for the people in your life that were not involved in your situation. For me PTSD did not stem from a single event in Afghanistan but a buildup of experiences, as well as a breakdown of my confidence in myself. Trust in myself started to gradually decline, and soon I was not myself anymore.

I had completed two separate year-long deployments in Iraq before my deployment to Afghanistan. Each deployment came with its own set of issues but Afghanistan was different. I talked to different people in the Army about PTSD, but it never really registered with me. In my second Iraq deployment, I found myself picking up body parts of a friend of mine that died when a car bomb went off in the streets of Jalawla, Diyala Province. Three Soldiers died and several got seriously hurt. The explosion was so big inside the VBIED (vehicle born improvised explosive device or "car bomb") that it launched the engine about 25 meters away. The side of the building next to that blast kind of reminded me of the *Iron Man 3* scene where Robert Downey, Jr. finds the spot where that local kid exploded. The civilians near him were cast onto a cinderblock wall the like shadows from a light. Some of the images of that day hung with me, but not to a point where I felt a need for those thoughts to be classified as PTSD, until I learned more about it.

None of the guys I had ever deployed with talked about PTSD, except to say that it was a bunch of shit. One NCO (Non-Commissioned Officer) of mine had been shot in the chest during a previous deployment of his and he seemed fine. Another NCO took a bullet to his helmet and he still seemed to function normally on a daily basis. When you heard about PTSD, you heard about people having mental breakdowns or crying for no reason. To me, PTSD had a stigma that made it sound like a crippling disorder making people unable to function in normal situations. It also seemed like there was a stigma in admitting you had PTSD. Not having experienced anything that could be classified as an extremely stressful situation, I felt like fixing any of those types of problems would be as easy as not thinking of them or just "manning up" and moving forward. Back then, I had never experienced anything that serious; nothing that would keep me awake at night; things that would make my blood start racing, skin start sweating, all because of a sound or a memory.

In 2011, my family and I got orders to move to Germany. My unit, 172nd Infantry Division, Task Force (TF) 3-66 Armor (AR), was based out of Grafenwoehr. I would spend about six months training with my unit before we deployed for Afghanistan, my third deployment and second with my wife and oldest son. The day I left was just as hard, if not harder, than the first time. My wife was as worried as ever with tears in her eyes as we said our good-byes near the parking lot. My oldest son (my second wouldn't be born until years later) was only four at the time and wasn't fully aware of the situation but could tell something was off because of the tears in his mother's eyes. Hugging my wife goodbye, I told her that this deployment would not be any different than before and I would call as soon as I could to let her know we made it safely to our destination.

After our good-byes, it was business as usual. Grab your bags, gear, weapon and move out. Something like three days later we would make it to our final outpost in Afghanistan. During our first few days in country, our unit made the advance to take back an enemy-controlled road into an over-run town. The push started late at night and lasted long into the next day. The road was lined with IEDs (Improvised Explosive Devices), and they were all followed with gun fire. As we made our slow push down the road, cleaning buildings and roadsides, one of our unit's trucks got hit by an IED. Sergeant Matthew Harmon and Corporal Joseph Vandreumel rushed to hook their wrecker up to the broken-down vehicle when another IED went off right under them. On August 14, 2011, they would be the first fatalities for TF 3-66 AR, three weeks into our year-long deployment.

The days during the deployment went by quickly. Our jobs kept us very busy from long three or four-day missions to missions that were as simple as driving to another COP (Command Out Post) and back. One mission went particularly long when an Afghan Army commander asked us to assist his troops with building a new COP, which also entailed providing 24-hour security during the effort. My platoon and I were tasked with conducting patrols of the area, during one of which we came under attack by rockets and mortars from the local fighters. I was standing on the ground next to my truck when the first mortar round landed. My gunner immediately returned fire in the direction of the SAF (Small Arms Fire) coming at us. Our M2 .50 cal machine guns started firing from all of our trucks while my soldiers on the ground gathered and started moving under the cover of friendly fire toward the enemy location. While some of us were standing along a wall, trading shots with the enemy, an RPG struck the opposite side and knocked us down. Our Afghan Army counterparts then released a volley of RPGs back in the direction of the enemy. By this time, the noise was so loud it was hard to talk with people I was standing right next to. A slight calm came over me at this point; no fear, no thoughts of death. I commanded mass fires on the enemy's location and advance as quickly as possible to gain ground on their location.

A day later, another platoon in our unit was doing a routine security patrol when one of their vehicles managed to get stuck. My platoon got tasked with assisting in recovery. As soon as we showed up and had the vehicle in sight, an RPG came out of nowhere, narrowly missing my truck. It landed and exploded to the back left of us. Instincts just kicked in at that point. We dismounted and deployed our teams out to find and destroy those stupid enough to take shots at us. Later that night, we were winding down, drinking some chai tea with the partnered Afghanistan Army Soldiers, when more rockets flew overhead and SAF started whipping all around us. Now, keep in mind that the COP we were building is in a very open field, about 300 meters from the walls of local city homes. It was very easy for them to shoot at us and run away. Lucky for us they did it at night. We were able to find them and finish that fight.

The reason why I am telling these events rather than just what happened to me is two-fold. The first one is to give you a sense of what happened during my Afghanistan deployment so you might better understand my state of mind. The second is because of the love and respect I have for all the soldiers, NCO's and officers I served with. Their stories are shared with mine. The more we talk about what we've seen or what we've gone through, the easier it becomes to escape the thoughts and overcome the ones you have the hardest time with. PTSD is the hardest when you feel alone, like you are the only one that might feel that way. These events in my life have changed me and without talking about them it might have changed me for the worse.

The day of my injury was a beautiful day in January 2012. I remember the air was cool but still manageable for January in the high mountains of Afghanistan. My mission that day was to escort our BC (Battalion Commander) to a local security meeting with the town's Afghan leaders. But, as my BC would say from time to time, "The enemy always has a vote too." Just before he came out to our convoy of trucks, we got word that a couple of fighters had shot a local police man and taken control of a communications building within the town. The building was also being used as an ammo supply area by the local police.

"Great," I said, "Now they have all the ammo they need to defend themselves."

Needless to say, the mission changed that day. An almost nine-hour fire fight ensued. After the firefight, an EOD (Explosive Ordinance Detachment) Team swept the building to make sure nothing was rigged to blow up on us. My guys and I went from room-to-room, floor-to-floor and identified all the shooters and the rooms they were lying in, dead. We did this to allow for the EOD team to clear the bodies of explosives, as well as to remove some of the grenades the fighters had used against us.

On the second day, my platoon was tasked with going back to the communications building to collect anything we could find on the bodies and in the rooms that might help learn who had sent these guys on their mission of death. Up to this point, I already had a few experiences with dead bodies on both sides of the fight. These bodies were getting gross. They smelled really bad and they seemed to be bloating. Their blood had dried after pooling around them. Flies that were buzzing around the bodies told us that the closer we got, the worse it would get. We decided to go to the second floor first, work our way back down and out from there. The room we started in had three dead guys in it. It was a right corner fed 20' x 30' or so sized room. There was a book case or two on the left wall and a table pushed up against the right wall. On the back wall, there was a window that took up a majority of the wall space, allowing in the sunlight that morning. The room was also lined with colorful rugs along with office-style furniture.

Before we started searching the room, I noticed one of the bodies was in the very same place it was yesterday, while the other two bodies had been rolled over and moved from their original spots. From this, I assumed that the unmoved body had not yet been checked or cleared by the EOD team the day before. For safety reasons, I had my team leave the room and planned to roll the body while my Senior Section Sergeant and good friend, Staff Sergeant (SSG) Celona, would stand in the door way, a safe distance away, and observe. I was standing over the body, with it between me and the doorway. I decided for safety I would lift the body up by its vest while still standing to allow me the space to run if need be. Boy, was I glad I did that. When I pulled the body up toward me so SSG Celona could see the underside, we heard a loud click... I quickly pushed the body back down, took two steps toward the door, but by the third step the body exploded.

The room went black. I couldn't hear anything for what felt like minutes. I also didn't feel any pain right away. The blast was strong enough to toss SSG Celona out of the doorway, slamming it closed while throwing half the contents of the room behind it. When I tried to stand, I could feel the pain shoot through my body. My legs and my arm were where it resonated first. After getting out of the room, my Doc (Medic) looked at my arm, bandaged it up and then bandaged the back of my head. I didn't even know my head was bleeding until he told me.

"We're going to need to get him back to the base," Doc told SSG Celona.

We gathered up the team and made our way out of the building and to our trucks. Sitting in the back of the truck, my arm started to tingle like that feeling you get when your arms or legs lose feeling due to blood being cut off to the nerves. It was only about a 20-minute convoy back to the base, but by then the pain in my body had doubled. My legs and back started to burn.

Once the truck stopped and the ramp dropped, my First Sergeant was there to help me into the base medical center. Everything happened very quickly once inside. Doctors told me that the blast sent bone fragmentation into my back, legs, and arm, ultimately hitting my ulnar nerve in my left arm. The arm was swelling up to the size of a wiffle ball bat and they needed to put me under general anesthesia in order to operate. Not 25 minutes earlier, I was knocked against a wall by a dead body and now these people wanted to put me out. I was so scared at that moment that I started to cry. I refused, but they responded with telling me it wasn't a discussion. They were just letting me know what they were going to do. They must have already administered the medicine because not long after that, I was out. Fast forward a few hours and I made it out of country and back to Germany where I would stay at Landstuhl Regional Medical Center. My wife made the drive to see me the next morning and while I recovered in the hospital, the Fisher House put her and my son up for free. It was an amazing show of support to families of injured soldiers.

I ended up needing five surgeries on my left arm. There is now a scare that is about three quarters of an inch at the widest point and runs from the center of my hand all the way down my forearm to my elbow. It took 37 stitches to hold it together. My right ear drum was perforated with a 33% hole and was later operated on as well. Both of my legs swelled to the point where I couldn't bend my knees. The bone shrapnel was pulled out of my back, legs, butt and head. Many tests would be done on my blood to ensure I didn't acquire any diseases. It took me 14 days until I was able to leave the hospital. During those days, I received a lot of therapy, both physical and psychological. The therapy sessions were not what I believe they should have been. They didn't last very long and didn't really get to the root of the issues. It would be almost a year before things got bad mentally.

On the April 1, 2012, I was on a plane back to Afghanistan to finish the deployment with my Platoon. I was welcomed with huge support, no one bigger than my BC, Lieutenant Colonel Curtis Taylor and Command Sergeant Major Dan Robinson. Without their guidance, leadership and support I would have never been able to finish the deployment. I can say that if I had not been able to finish with my Soldiers, to walk off that plane at the end of the deployment, rather than being carried on a stretcher, I would have been worse off mentally than I feel like I am.

The weight of what happened wouldn't really show itself until more time had passed. Back in Afghanistan, things felt normal; missions went on just as before. I did feel a bit different when I thought a situation might turn ugly, but I tried to suppress that feeling as if it was only the fear I was used to, and not the actual events taking place in front of me. After the deployment ended things felt like normal until everyday life stresses started to happen. Every day activities like grocery shopping, washing dishes, making dinner, driving, etc. seemed to become a bigger issue than it needed to be. Although these stresses happened before during previous deployments, this time was different. Being in a grocery store and feeling confined would cause me to just walk out, leaving a full grocery cart in the middle of the aisle. The stress wouldn't leave either. It just compounded and made me feel like there was no way of ending it, so I started drinking more... and more.

I would drink at home where I felt I could control the situation. In social situations where I am out with friends, I find myself holding back. Especially in the places that are new to me. Watching everyone's mannerisms, watching the door. I don't let myself get too loose in public. My emotions around large groups of people have changed over the years. In stores and shopping malls I feel claustrophobic, like I'm not in control of what is happening or could be happening. Sitting in a bar, I watch people move, how different group's interactions shift, how much people are drinking, when people leave the room and who follows them. I haven't turned it off. It makes me uncomfortable to be in those situations, but I do it anyway because the people I'm with are friends and I should be safe.

There are times when I feel like I can't act like myself in large groups of people. The looks I get make me feel uncomfortable and misunderstood. Most of the time I just keep my mouth closed and my opinions to myself. The way I talk to my Army friends and the interactions I still have with them allow me to feel a part of a group. Feeling cut off from social situations is a hard thing to deal with. I sit here now, writing this while in the basement of a home that is full of people for a Christmas party. I feel transparent to them. Here is a group that I'm a part of, but feel like I don't belong; a group of people and a place I've grown up in that now feels cold and foreign. Then I realize that it's not the place. It's not the people around me. I've come to the understanding that it's me. I've changed in ways people can't comprehend. I'm trapped in a box that I cannot get out of and no one can help.

The choice I made to have my Soldiers leave the room prior to me rolling the body saved them from being injured and possibly killed, but did I make the best choice overall? Couldn't I have just left the body and moved on, or maybe tied rope to it and pulled it over (which is how I teach everyone to do it now)? Dozens of different choices could have been made that day with dozens of different outcomes. Did the best one come out or did I make a bad call? These questions still linger in my head years later. The worst part about it all is how I see the injury and myself. I made a bad choice that resulted in the injury of myself and my good friend. Thank God we didn't get more hurt than we did, which brings me to another point: why should I feel so bad about what happened to me? I still have the use of all my limbs. Soldiers are coming home missing eyes, legs, arms and here I am feeling sorry for myself... fuck no! I won't let myself feel bad. My injuries are so small on the scale that they shouldn't even register. So, for years, I would trap my emotions and tell myself that nothing really happened to me, demand of myself to harden the fuck up and drive on, tell myself that much worse has happened to other people so quit feeling sorry for yourself and move out.

BUILDING BLOCKS TO BREAK THEM DOWN

Grant Rogers

Born and raised in Louisiana, we didn't have much growing up. Dad worked two jobs while going to school, and Mom worked her job. They shared a 1987 Buick that was dark, ugly and brown, with the ceiling falling out of it. We would put tacks in it to hold the car ceiling from sagging. Dad would ride his bike to work and would eventually get a little blue S-10 Chevrolet pick-up. We lived in a hand-me-down trailer and didn't need much. Growing up had its challenging times. I struggled in school and got held back in the first grade. School was boring for me. I was always thinking about something and creating ideas in my head. If you were to ask me then if I'd be writing a book today, I would have laughed in your face or asked you to repeat the question. Growing up, I always wanted to find out the reason behind something and how it worked, what made it tick and what it really was. A lot of my friends defined people by how much money their parents made or what car they drove. Looking back, I wouldn't have changed my life for the world. The greatest wealth my family provided was love, and for that, I am forever grateful.

When I was about 4 years old, Dad and I would build blocks up tall, and then I would knock them all down, only to build them back up again. I didn't get to see him as much as I would have liked, because he was in the military. I grew up around the military and didn't even realize it at the time. A grandfather, great grandfather and an uncle served. One was a paratrooper with the 82nd Airborne Division, another was in the 456th AAA Battalion, Field Artillery that shot down fighter planes in WW2 and my great uncle was a paratrooper in the 101st Airborne. One had drinking problems and hit my great-grandmother. Another was quiet, stern, never talked about the war and when asked, silence came over his face with a dull stare. He would say things like, "Son, never ask me about war again." Now, let's fast forward. I was going through high school and was bored, downright bored. I loved baseball and played other sports to keep my mind busy. While walking through the mall one day, I was approached by an Army recruiter. I went home and told my Mom. She was a bit shocked, but I had already made up my mind that I was going.

Ring... Ring... Ring.

"Dad, I'm at the Army recruiting station."

"You're what?"

"Yeah dad, I just need a waiver and need you to sign it."

"Um, OK, let me talk to your recruiter."

Talk about an impulse decision. At the time, it felt right. I wanted an escape, something new in my life, an adventure and boy would I get one. The day before I left for basic I got a call from Dad.

"Do you remember when you were little and we would build those blocks up and then you would knock all of them down just to build them back up again?

"Yes, sir, I sure do."

"Well, you are about to get a lot of blocks knocked off and it isn't going to feel good, but in due time you will be built up and no one and nothing will be able to knock you down again."

I laughed it off, "OK, Dad, whatever, I love you. Goodnight."

My dad had substance and depth in his advice and always has. It's because he cares and little did I know I was about to enter a world where everyone came from a diverse background. For some of them, it was the first family they ever had. Something my dad wouldn't be able to prepare me for, nor would anyone else, would be the aftermath of war. I had all the blocks, but had to put the pieces together on my own. These are the blocks that make me who I am today: a leader, a mentor, a coach, a warrior. Did I think that I could have died out there? Of course. But with time, that faded. Also, I trusted the guys to my left and right. You don't always trust everyone you serve with, but I trusted them and still do to this very day! My recruiters said it would be like college: women, booze and freedom away from mom and dad's house. Hell, more like women in spurts, booze galore on the weekend and freedom. That's what we would all be fighting for.

Basic training and Advanced Individual Training was a blur, so I will skip that and move to the more intriguing part of becoming a lean, mean, green, fighting machine. Growing up in the Army was a blast. We worked hard to play harder as a team, as a family, as brothers. We had each other's back and then some. That was the beauty of brotherhood. But, how did we get to that point? We earned it. From competing in physical fitness to drinking the last drop of alcohol, everything was a competitive challenge. We lost our names, and they were replaced with FNGs (Fucking New Guys) or DICK (Deadly Individual Combat Killer). It took about 6 months for us to earn the right to be called by our last names, let alone having rank placed in front of it. These times were grueling and made me think to myself, *what the hell have I gotten myself into*? Looking back, I got myself into something that I will never regret, and I found out who I was for, what I am, and what I'm not. I've learned who others are, who others said they were and who they really aren't. It's not about the war anymore, it's about the look on the post-face next to the pre-face. I'll explain. Looking back, you give up everything. You give up your high school car, sweetheart, friends, sports etc. For what? The unknown, the unexpected and the darkness, without seeing the light. Going into it all was fun, challenging, different and unique. It was like no other experience in the world. My first duty assignment was Ft. Lewis, Washington, at 1-14 Cavalry.

"Here you go, Private. Unload your shit and wait one."

What does "wait one" even mean? Alright, I just had to "wait one" and stand there with my "shit." Well, I waited 30 ones. Those were a long 30 ones. Then the barracks windows creaked open with disgruntled men looking down on me.

"Look boys, fresh meat! Ha-ha-hah ha-ha-ha! Yeah, welcome to the suck, GUY!"

This was all very intriguing. I wasn't even awake yet from the plane ride. Two years of extensive training for combat operations in Iraq had commenced and we were hungry. The thought of dying, the thought of never seeing my family again, and the thought of killing someone was relevant but ignored, avoided and dismissed. I was a fucking machine. We were all built up this way. None of those thoughts ever entered my mind until my weapon went hot, chambering a round and rolling outside the wire. I didn't care if someone shot at us. If they tried to blow us up, I didn't care. I cared about the guys, I cared about the mission and I cared about getting back home. Family became more and more distant. I had a new family now, or so it felt that way. As I would travel the world and go to different duty stations, I would miss previous persons I had served with. I had to reestablish my name, my trust and my soldiering as a person each time I was around like-minded soldiers. But it never got easier. It just got more difficult as I would miss the bonds that were created along the way.

PTSD/PTS

Post-traumatic stress disorder or post-traumatic stress is something I never knew anything about. The likeness of having it was rare and all was good, or so I thought. I avoided getting help for about 3 years, however when I went to get help, I got the run around: You need to see the TBI (Traumatic Brain Injury) clinic. You need to see mental health. You need to see someone. No shit. Because I didn't get a definitive answer, I continued to avoid and soldiered through it. It would catch up to me in drinking, women, and being reckless with my life. I had started a downhill trend that I didn't recognize, I didn't look myself in the mirror and see who I was becoming, but my shadow saw the entire thing, and has seen everything from day one. It cornered me into a room with a mental health professional. It was the unknown for me.

I wondered how this person could relate, what did they know about me and my brothers and what we've been through?

I would later be told how I was "broken" and would start to constructively put the pieces of me back together. One by one, piece by piece. It wasn't easy and still isn't to this day, but I work on it day-in and day-out. A portion of therapy that I went through was IOP (Intensive Outpatient Program) PTSD/Combat related in San Antonio, Texas. Some have suggested that it is the "cure all" for PTSD. Although it did help me, I don't believe it is the cure all. I firmly believe that doctors want it to be a cure all so that they can attract more people to come for rehab to further analyze it. They've changed the name of PTSD/PTS so many times based off of case studies, and research, but the majority haven't gone through it or aren't facing it. In therapy, they just go off textbook answers and apply it accordingly. During my therapy, the Doctor told me in a group session that it will eventually go away. I stated, "I beg to differ." He obliged and asked that I explain.

"The way I see it, is that it's a wound that needs healing treatments and stitched together. After taking care of it, it will become a scar, a scar for life."

"Very good insight and I like that analogy," he replied. "I've never heard that before."

So, in my opinion, I was put in a catch 22 type of situation. He asked me to explain so that I would participate and so he could put a physiological spin on it. I summed therapy up to me becoming mentally broken from all the training and "brainwashing" I had received. They really were trying to reverse some of my mind and what I had been taught. It was working. I would later find out that a thought is much

195

different than a feeling. My feelings were helplessness, rage, scared, numb, confused, guilt, and loneliness and vulnerable. My thoughts were posed as I am. So, I wrote down that I am lost, denied, not in control, not a tough guy, don't know who I am and worthless to society. These all became apparent in my mind due to an event. There are many events in our life that can cause traumas. These traumas go untreated or medicine is thrown at them. Not everyone has to go to war to be a "victim" of post-traumatic stress. Most of us experience a trauma at a young age and we grow into an adult based on our life choices, experiences and different situations that we face daily as human beings.

Whether you are 30 or 60 years of age, whenever you experienced a traumatic event, that is the exact moment those events, thoughts and feelings are essentially captured. They fester and can be triggered at other times in our lives. Deep down, we are still children. We are still that 10-year-old little boy that was left in the driveway by his father who stayed gone for 10 years. We may be a 10-year-old little girl who was abused physically or mentally and now as an adult, certain actions trigger you or make you feel unsafe. The point is, the healing never begins until we are mindful of what triggers us and what doesn't. We shouldn't just avoid everything and anything. This feeds depression, anxiety and fears. It grabs you by the back, and brings you down full-force every day. You become belligerent with life, people, and lose interests in doing things you used to enjoy. I know I did, and so have many others. I often would drink, to "ease the pain" or it would take me back to "feeling normal." But, all it did was bring me to a nirvana state-of-mind, which I thoroughly enjoyed, even though the come-down was brutal. I became a mute and didn't want to move. It was self-destructive and not productive whatsoever. I used to get so drunk, I would wake up and start clearing rooms and other things I'd rather not mention. I would wake up the next morning and not have a clue what I had done. I was scaring the shit out of myself and everyone else.

Eventually, I started doing things that interested me, like sports, fitness, music, and art. Baseball found me again and

I haven't left it since. The smell of fresh cut grass, the lights, and ambience of it all is captivating. To play the game I love with other veterans who get me and I get them is therapeutic for me. It reconnects the disconnect that I've faced since being taken away from the people I served with. It is very hard to pack up and move on, over and over again. That's the military life and it creates a distant type of mindset. A mindset where you don't allow yourself to get attached to things or people anymore. Baseball and other sports have brought back some of the connections that I've had along the way. It's a beautiful thing. I have transformed my feelings and anger into the weights I lift. When transitioning that anger, it came out as a positive result for me. I got fat because I lost all motivation, but I started to re-create my body and the definition it had.

Music drives my being. It exhilarates me and allows me to have a creative thinking process. I do this daily, if I'm feeling down. What I don't do is listen to hate music or yelling/screaming music, unless I'm working out. When I drive, I listen to calm, soothing music. It allows for less road rage and a calmer approach to idiotic situations on the highway.

Art allows me to express my thoughts to reflect back to me from a canvas. I was never a good artist; however, seeing a scrambled mind come out on a canvas is beautiful. You get to see and express your thoughts that others are or may be going through at the time. Once it is all there in front of you, you start to see balance. That balance is needed in life to be anything and everything we want to be. Otherwise, you spend your time on so much of the wrong things. After sifting through the bullshit, you come to the final answer. And, that answer is you! I believe that we should all complement our personalities with things that complement them back. What we are born to do has been tucked away deep, deep down the entire time. Invest in yourself so that others will be attracted to the overall goal in life: Living! I wrote a letter to myself at the end of therapy while sitting on the hillside of mountainous terrain...

"Therapy today, writing this to myself as a goal. I hope you find

197

happiness, love, and a new life. I hope that new life is fulfilled with many blessings and a beautiful journey!" I am still on that journey today and it's getting more beautiful by the second.

In my opinion, a trauma is not a choice, it's an event. That event brings about feelings and then thoughts. People often get the two confused or they are misinterpreted.

28 February 2010 QRF (Quick Reaction Force):

"X-Ray, trucks are at red com one."

"White Platoon, we need you to move out."

We move out on a hazy day, with the smell of death in the air. Sifting through our senses and piercing our minds was a sixth sense that kicked in; something just felt off. I didn't feel right. Just like the time I was 10 years old in the driveway... waiting. Singing a song as to why my Dad left me sitting there.

I dismount with three men, I'm the two-man in the stack, and we're going into the courtyard. I felt the fire rush through my flesh. **BOOM**! I go black. My mouth chalky with a deep sense of confusion. I saw a different world. I hear yelling and gunfire raining out. I check my body sporadically for blood. The adrenaline hit me like a freight train. What was this feeling? My body absorbing the wave of the explosion. My vision going in and out along with my hearing of nothing but ringing. I came to, grabbed my weapon and started checking on everyone.

"What was your first traumatic experience?"

I laugh and then say, "Oh, it was February 28, 2010. I was dismounted and got hit by my first IED."

"And your feelings... What were they? Oh, and what about your thoughts now?"

I've been exposed. Shit! They all see exactly who I am, but why can't I see who I am? Why am I struggling to see it?

The group all raised their hands except for the ones that had been through combat. Combat or not, that wasn't the point. The point was I was avoiding these thoughts, feelings and emotions. Or in laymen's terms, PTSD!

I didn't have it. Nope, not me, no way! We were always taught admitting to problems was a sign of weakness and no one had time for weak blood on the team. Perspective. It put a lot of perspective out there for me, the therapy that is. It helped bring every single thing full circle. As I sat there detoxing, I felt the energy all around me. I felt the hate, the disgrace, the wounded traumas and emotions of others. Gut wrenching, really, all of it. The rape victims, the identity victims, the silent victims that you could see straight through. Funny, they were doing the same thing to me. I would constantly ask myself "Why? Why this? Why that?"

Truth be told, asking why just frustrates the ever-living shit out of me. I want to know why, and knowing why without them telling me, drives me insane. I now look in the mirror and talk to myself. Crazy, I know. But I reflect and it reflects back. It's embarrassing to face myself. I guess that's why I avoided doing it so much in the past and didn't even know what I was avoiding. When I do look in the mirror, I see what the world sees... me! In the past, I would just look at every one of them instead of myself. "Hey, fucking private, how about you drop and beat your face."

This is what I was being fed, and this is what creates a war machine. I would later inflict those same styles on my soldiers. I was an animal inside, I wanted my men alive and not in some box shipped back home to mom and dad. They didn't understand, and neither did I.

Carbine Addiction

As the smoke of the carbine sifts through the air, my head swivels looking for more imminent danger, living life like an ongoing dare. I fiend for adrenaline, a rush to the head, addicted to pumping the trigger twice, not thinking I could be dead. The adrenaline is what kept me alive, it's what kept me fed. The smell of the carbine left on my skin, pierced my sense deeply and forever ongoing sin. As the smoke of the carbine sifts through the air!

The day I received my DD-214 was the day I was looking forward to for a very long time. After that day, the time started to really tick, I entered the "civilian life" of everyday chaos. I say chaos because I had not seen this world since I was 17, and even then, didn't really get a chance to be acquainted with that lifestyle. I contradicted myself. I stated that I disliked the civilian life and the way people lived, yet I wanted to be a part of it so badly. At the end of the day, I knew that it wasn't anyone else's fault, responsibility or obligation to start accomplishing things in my life. Before I would begin to take that first step, I would stay up late into the early hours of the morning, not being able to sleep. I would think about the past and how I missed it. I missed the people I served with. The times that I did have a traumatic experience replayed in my mind, it wasn't like a paranoid replay, but a sense of feeling it like it was yesterday that I also miss. I was, and still am, getting older. So, essentially my body was just in motion but my mind was stuck in the past. I was just going through the motions of life, not really paying any attention to goals, people or things. I had lost interests. I felt like I pushed a lot of limits already and survived so much, so why not live carelessly? Why not give up and just say "Fuck it?"

I would lay in bed, isolate myself, and stay delved into my phone, only to go back to sleep again. This was such a downward spiral, that I was searching for happiness through others, only to exhaust their being and then move on to the next person looking for the same things again. These things include, acceptance, justification, love, help, and happiness.

Where had it all gone? I would later find out that it was staring right in front of me the entire time, I just wasn't man enough to face it! You've got to start facing your problems and be exposed to the things that trouble you. My mind goes in so many different places with ideas, views and the existence of living. I was running from myself and trying to fill those voids of doubt and self-identity. This was bullshit. How could I go from fighting on different continents to completely isolating myself, from everything?

Security in life, security in driving, security in walking, security in war. It's fragile, just like our minds are fragile. They can be easily effected by traumas. Does that mean we give up? Does that mean we turn to self-aiding alternatives to mask the issues at hand? Can we trust people or things anymore? It's hard to determine that if you are not mindful or self-reflecting and really taking a deep look at who you are in this life. For me, all of the above has allowed for growth and judgment. I believe that victims of trauma can be a very powerful, positive force in inducing growth. We've got to quit allowing ourselves to fall and then blaming it on others. We have to pick up our ruck or backpack of emotions and head up that hill. We will not win every battle or problem along the way. But as long as at the end of our journey we win the war and conquer life, that's something to have lived for and through.

I encourage you. Whether you've experienced hard times, ongoing traumatic events or day-to-day setbacks, pick your life up and be an aspirational success story that saves people through your own positive influence. Through your self-purpose in life, rest assured, it will become addicting and persons will follow. In life, we play multiple roles with co-workers, with spouses, and with people, in general. When I have to act differently or obscure my personality, I feel like I'm lying and being someone that I'm not. When people say things that trigger me, I'm not myself, so I just remain quiet or walk away. When in all actuality, I want to tell them exactly how I feel about them and about the situation, period. That, however, is not politically correct and quite frankly I don't care anymore. I am who I am. What makes me myself is self-regulation. If I don't regulate my impulses, then I will spin out of control, only to find emptiness. It will feel good at the moment, but at the end it is bare. In my opinion, a lot of people that experience traumas don't channel positive energy. They usually blame others or want to get payback. I challenge you to seek help, understand your emptiness and conquer life one goal at a time. Those of us who have faced "the fear" are the ones who can live life and begin to start winning. Facing "the fear" is what gives us the edge in life. It's what drives that inner spark.

"White ONE Eagle" ... Out!

BACK FROM THE BRINK

Dana Brown

  My journey in the U.S. Army started in January 2005. But, before you hear about that story you need to know where I came from and how I ended up there. I grew up in New England and lived mostly around the North Shore and Cape Cod areas of Massachusetts, as well as the coastal region near Portland, Maine. I had some other stops across the country at times due to my father serving 30 years in the U.S. Coast Guard, but New England was always home. Growing up, I was a typical kid who liked cars, hanging out on the beach, exploring the mountains and woods, and playing ice hockey. I never thought about joining the U.S. military until I was a sophomore in college. The typical path of graduating high school and attending college was pushed on me pretty hard by my parents and society, in general. Honestly, I got sick and tired of all of it. I had a friend who enlisted in the U.S. Army and left for Fort Benning, Georgia, literally hours after graduating high school. For him, the Army was a way to escape from Maine, see the world and earn some money for college. After a few months, I finally got to reconnect with him and I heard about his adventures with the 1st Ranger Battalion and a deployment to Iraq. He told me about the good things and perks of being a soldier, as well as some of the bad things (Matt, if you're reading this, you never told me about CQ and Staff Duty and not to mention all of the BS safety training, but I'm assuming Rangers don't worry about that stuff).

  As I was becoming increasingly bored in college, I started to research certain jobs in the military. I looked at jobs in the Marines, such as Light Armored Crewman and Infantry. I looked at the Army and its jobs, such as Cavalry Scout, Infantry, and Armor Crewman. At first it was just random research spurred by curiosity. After a while, though, I needed to find a calling or a purpose in life, and if I was to join the military, I wanted to actually fight rather than be in a support position. Nothing against that, but it wasn't for me. The war in Iraq was starting to pick up with operations in Fallujah all over the news and seeing Marines and Soldiers fighting house-to-house kind of made me feel like I was missing out on my generation's great crusade against terrorism. I asked my father about the military more and more. As I thought back to growing up as a military brat, I saw some great things that helped influence my decision to join the military. So, right before Christmas in 2004, I went to the Army recruiter and MEPs (Military Entrance Processing), signed a "liberty contract" of two and half years and left for basic training to become a Cavalry Scout at Fort Knox, Kentucky. My mom was pretty upset that her only child dropped out of college and enlisted in the Army during a time of war in a position that would put me on the front lines. My father was pretty proud, but I think inside he would have rather had me enlist in the Coast Guard and drive surf boats.

Fast forward some months and I was graduating from Fort Knox as a Cavalry Scout, eager to jump on a Bradley Fighting Vehicle and kick-in doors to find the bad guys. Except my career path was not what normal Cavalry Scouts follow. During my first few years I was in a light infantry company that doubled as honor guard for the United Nations Command in South Korea, then I was in an Armored Cavalry Troop that trained and acted the part of an opposing force for future Army and Marine Armor officers, and I even spent time in a quick reaction security element alongside military police at Fort Knox. Needless to say, my first three years in the Army were not as advertised, especially considering all of my battle buddies from basic training had already been to Iraq or Afghanistan at least once. When reenlistment came up, I decided to ask for the Army's new "go-to" unit: 2nd Infantry Division's Stryker Brigade. This unit pioneered the light armor tactics in urban terrain and blended light infantry operations with reconnaissance on the battlefield.

I arrived at Fort Lewis, Washington, right as the 3rd Stryker Brigade came home from a 15-month deployment to Iraq. After being in for three years and seeing the light infantry and armored side of the cavalry I thought I knew everything. Well, I was wrong about that. At Fort Lewis, I fell under some outstanding NCOs and to this day, I had the best section leaders I ever served under. To me, these guys were legends in the cavalry community, taking a new vehicle platform that was unproven and tactics that were usually reserved for infantry units and combined them with reconnaissance operations. When these guys spoke, you listened and took notes, because they were teaching you how to survive on the battlefield. If you didn't, some of the iron-willed team leaders would make sure you did. I was assigned to Headquarters Troop as a gunner for the Squadron Commander (SCO) and the Command Sergeant Major. Most of the time, it was a pretty decent job. I got to know far more about the Squadron than I wanted to know, but I still got to go train with Crazy Horse Troop and Bronco Troop when they conducted ranges or other exercises. After being at Fort Lewis for two years, I got to finally go on a Middle Eastern Safari to scenic Iraq. For 12 months, we would train and advise the Iraqi military on how to conduct counter insurgency operations in a contentious area that had some of the last insurgent strong holds in the country. I was amped-up and ready to go kick in doors, but it didn't quite go that way. During the first few months, we drove to a lot of key leader engagements where the SCO would talk about security, how to develop better relations with the Kurdish military in the north and how to use money from the Department of State to build better schools and roads. While I was dealing with this, the rest of the squadron was out chasing bad guys, training the joint Iraqi-Peshmerga security force and hitting the occasional IED. The squadron had taken two losses at this point, but I didn't know the men since they were attachments to our unit. I felt that the scouts and infantry were on their game and that nothing catastrophic could happen. Then June 10, 2010 hit roughly 28 days before our lead elements started to fly home to the States.

June 10th started out like any normal day for us. We woke up at 0600 to go eat breakfast, then worked on the trucks and waited to see if the SCO had a meeting or something going on. The first hint that we had a platoon in trouble was when my driver, our medic and I were walking to check on the trucks and two Strykers came hauling ass past us. Then, we saw Bronco Troop's QRF (Quick Reaction Force) take off as a friend of mine in that platoon yelled from his truck that one of the platoons from Crazy Horse Troop got hit and two soldiers were missing. When an IED attack or a small arms engagement happens, it's very easy for a soldier to be unaccounted for in the chaos. It's usually because of a communications issue, but this time it wasn't. Reports on the ground were that the body armor was found at one location while a radio and rifle were found at another location. Body parts were recovered, but from the QRF's assessment, one man was still missing. To this day, I don't know who was buried under the rubble of a collapsed building in that market, but I do know that we didn't leave that area for 18 hours, when we recovered that soldier's remains.

My section was slowly snaking its way through narrow alleys and side streets to try to clear areas and see if we could find the attackers. We had no luck. Eventually, we ended up on the far side of the market and established perimeter security before dismounting with the SCO to try and see what happened. The platoon that got hit was Gold platoon from the 5th Battalion, 20th Infantry, known as The Regulars. They were attached to our Crazy Horse Troop to give them greater numbers and enable them to execute more patrols and missions. We pulled up into the area and helped the QRF establish more security as the SCO got on the ground to assess what happened. When the ramp of my truck dropped, the first thing I saw when I got on the ground was a bag of Cheetos with fingers and the remnants of a hand nearby... that's an image I'll never forget.

The market was a scene out of a movie: buildings collapsed, a huge crater in the ground, blood and the remains of people and cars everywhere. I walked alongside the SCO and provided security for him as we walked around the market. I talked to a couple of the guys from Bronco Troops QRF (Quick Reaction Force) and it was kind of like a shock and awe factor. Here we are 28 days from some of us going home and we're picking up the remains and equipment of our infantry brothers. We spent hours roaming around the area trying to figure out what happened and why. Eventually, we found out that a squad from this platoon was baited down an alley towards this market and a 1200-pound car bomb exploded when they got near it. They ended up losing two soldiers and had several wounded.

The images of that day triggered something in me that I couldn't explain. During the deployment, I was always on guard and looking out for anything that could harm my truck and myself. However, we were a happy-go-lucky bunch. Now, I thought every car was going to explode and that my driver and dismounts were becoming complacent. My guys can attest that during the last month in country, I became a dick. I was always up their asses about stupid stuff and riding them hard even though they were doing an amazing job. The chaplain came and talked to all of the units that were at the market that day. Talking about the events from my perspective did help me deal with it. Maybe it's because we were so wrapped up in getting ready to head home that I never thought about it or had issues until I came home.

The first couple days that I was home, things were pretty good. I spent time with my girlfriend and proposed to her and went on many adventures in Seattle. Since I was on orders to Fort Carson, Colorado, I really had no responsibility for anything in the section since I was getting ready to transfer. Needless to say, that without a truck, and a crew to take care of, I had a lot of time on my hands. Then things started to happen slowly at first. I became very irritated with little things that happened here and there, such as the dishwasher being loaded wrong or the laundry not being folded. I had difficulty sleeping and didn't really care about things that I used to enjoy. I ended up having an attitude at work with my platoon sergeant. I would tell my fiancé (who later became my ex-wife) some pretty mean things that started some arguments. To deal with this, I started to drink excessively. It wasn't a couple beers either. It was a bottle of whiskey a night, which kind of numbed the world around me and all of my feelings. After work, I'd come home and start slamming a bottle of whiskey and shut myself out of the world. The worst part to me, is that no one seemed to care. Before I transferred, I had to go to a post deployment health assessment where they asked you a ton of questions for mental and physical health based on your deployment. For the mental health questions, I raised some eyebrows on a lot of them, but I was given the "toughen up" treatment and brushed to the side. At the time, I didn't think I was that messed up in the head. Looking back, I know for a fact the excessive drinking and the way I talked to my wife was leading down a destructive path where I could have hurt myself or others. For about three months I was like this and it seemed like a normal day in my world.

After being back in the States for about four months, my wife and I moved from Washington to Colorado. Things were up and down with me, and I figured I had my bad days like everyone else. When I arrived at Fort Carson, I was given an incoming medical evaluation and the doctors saw the post deployment assessment from Iraq and immediately put me into a behavioral rehabilitation program. They were shocked that I wasn't in treatment since developing destructive behavior and continued to work every day. The Behavioral Rehab Program at Fort Carson did an amazing job of getting me back on track and if they wouldn't have helped me, I might not be telling my story right now. Three times a week I talked to my counselor about the events of that day in Iraq and how life was afterwards. For me, talking about it certainly helped a lot and it was nice to know that help was always there. Through the program, I stopped drinking and spent more time trying to be a better soldier and husband. The only thing I didn't like with the program was that I was put on two types of prescribed drugs. One helped, but the other had pretty bad side effects. The one with bad side effects was a drug to help me sleep, which it did, but after I took it I couldn't remember certain things that happened at night. I couldn't even remember letting my dogs out before bed or having sex with my wife. After a few months of this I had enough and slowly stopped taking them. I don't think the rehab program was trying to harm me, but the sleep aid had unforeseen consequences.

By this time, I had been back from Iraq for a little over a year and things were going a lot better. I earned a section leader slot in my platoon's Bradley section and I was developing myself as a better leader by completing several college courses and some NCO professional development courses. On a personal level I started to enjoy things that I used to do before Iraq, like building Subaru's into weekend track cars and go camping and fishing with some guys from my unit. Life was going pretty well.

In December 2011, my brigade was chosen to deploy advisory teams to Southern Afghanistan to support the NATO (North Atlantic Treaty Organization) fight down there. I figured, "why not?" And, volunteered to go see another country. Of all my time overseas, I'll say that Afghanistan was the worst. Those nine months were some of the toughest I ever faced in my entire life. We dealt with a lot of political BS in how to develop a program to empower the Afghan Police to conduct security operations, a battalion that we were attached to who didn't care about us at all, and our platoon-sized outpost had resupply issues. At times, it was how I imagine living on Mars would be. Oh, by the way, did I mention fighting season? Being assigned the Panjwei district was almost like a death sentence in some regards. This area was the home of the Taliban where they developed new tactics and fought Americans daily to gain experience and knowledge before they headed off into the Helmand or over to RC (Regional Command) East (Eastern Afghanistan). Every time a dismounted patrol went out, it was almost expected that someone would step on a pressure plate IED or a fire fight would occur. From May to October, our lives consisted of roaming around the district as a battle taxi. As scouts, we knew how to operate trucks with heavy crew-served weapons and had a great grasp on maneuvering in a fight. One of the company's we worked closely with was Bayonet Company, 1-64 Armor from Fort Stewart, Georgia. These guys were damn good warfighters who gave the Taliban hell every day in the Sperwan Ghar area. We developed a pretty good relationship with them. They patrolled the grape fields and we patrolled the roads. Every day when they walked out the gate to conduct patrols, we were driving our trucks on routes in the area with our Afghan counterparts to help support, if needed. One of the daily events that we dealt with was the MEDEVAC (Medical Evacuation) missions for our Afghan counterparts. Once fighting season hit you could count on having to do about three to four MEDEVACs a week. Essentially our counter parts would get wounded in a firefight or IED attack and they would rush to our COP, so we could treat them, get them on a helicopter for further care in Kandahar.

At first, these MEDEVACS weren't too bad. However, when we started to treat more civilians then our counterparts it got a little difficult. We were treating kids who were playing in a field and stepped on an IED. We must have been doing OK since most of the MEDEVACs we executed were successful and our counterparts and the locals survived.

During fighting season was when I was hit with a lot of bad things all at once. My wife left me for another soldier on Fort Carson, a couple of good friends were wounded and sent home, and two really good friends of mine were killed. All of this hit me like a ton of bricks. It was difficult to deal with as we were still doing our daily missions and patrols. My platoon sergeant and my medic saw early-on that I was dealing with a lot of these issues and that my mental state was slipping. At first, we had little talks about life when we would get back to the States; things to do and not to do. These little talks helped a lot and kept my head above water. I was pretty much told that when I got back I couldn't drink and start a destructive pattern similar to what I did after Iraq. My medic was the one who really got on my case and helped me distance myself from these issues. Doc started to use me as his personal assistant for medical classes and our escapades in cooking spam and anything else laying around since we had a supply issue. Another thing that helped me a little bit to was how our COP adopted a small cat that we named Zombie. Whenever you went to the gym or to sit outside on a bench, Zombie would jump up and sit next to you and comfort you just like a dog or cat would back home. Between the support of the guys on my team and this little cat, the future of going back looked a lot brighter.

When I got back to the States, I found out that my soon to be ex-wife had trashed my house and pretty much left my dog on his own. My dog, Brizzie, and I decided to help out each other as we rebuilt our house. I don't know how to explain it but in that time frame working on my house was kind of therapeutic and Brizzie was my best friend. The time together bonding kind of told me that everything would be OK. This time I decided to attack the problem head-on and reenrolled in the behavioral rehabilitation program. For five months, I met with a counselor who listened and helped me deal with my issues. Upon coming home, I still had issues sleeping, felt like I was being watched, and was always on alert. Brizzie slept on the bed with me and if he knew that I was having a rough time he would come up and cuddle with me or if we were out in public, he would immediately sit down and force me to pet him. He was acting like an unofficial PTSD support dog and he certainly helped me a lot. Brizzie also became the unofficial barrack's mascot when I had to make weekend barracks checks.

During the two and half years after Afghanistan, I started to look for other ways to enjoy life and put my issues with PTSD behind me. One of the biggest things that helped was the sense of adventure. I took my jeep wrangler and loaded it down with camping equipment and would go explore the mountains of Colorado in search of old ghost towns and places to fly fish. I would take Brizzie on these adventures and our time together made me forget about some of the horrors and push past things that held me back in the past. The whole adventure thing also spurred a love for Enduro motorcycles. I ended up joining a group of Enduro riders in Colorado who were all veterans. During our rides, we would help each other out with our PTSD issues and what worked and didn't work for us since everyone deals with things differently. This group of guys provided help and support that a counselor or a rehab program couldn't and our love of taking motorcycles up into the mountains of Colorado provided an escape from reality.

I walked away from the U.S. Army at almost 12 years of service, during which I had deployed for a total of 36 months, primarily in the Middle East and Central Asia. I met some amazing people along the way and everyone has their own story. The two deployments I just talked about here were two of the most difficult periods of my life. Of my four total deployments, those two were by far the most interesting as well. I hope my story helps out someone to the point that they aren't alone out there. I look at the treatment that I received for PTSD as both conventional and unconventional. I went with the normal conventional route of talking to counselors and being medicated which worked in some aspects. Then, I started to look for the unconventional route and that led me to a support group of veteran motorcyclists and my loyal dog who was always by my side.

It's been eight months since I took off my uniform for the last time and the transition is still new to me. Since I've been out of the military, and have been treated for issues from PTSD, I have remarried an amazing girl and we have expanded our family to three Australian Cattle Dogs. They always keep me on my toes and kind of make me feel like I'm running a fire team again. I ride my motorcycle in search of new trails and missing parts of our history in the northern woods of Minnesota. I'm currently working on finishing my bachelor's degree in business management and am considering pursuing my masters. If I wouldn't have received the help and support years ago I might not be writing this right now and possibly could have been a statistic. To me the biggest part in dealing with PTSD is accepting help and that help is similar to a MEDEVAC Blackhawk landing on a hot landing zone in parts unknown.

~ Valkyrie 15 ~

This concludes Chalk Three.

KEEP IT AFLAME

Where do we go from here?

THIS WILL NEVER BE OUR WEAKNESS

K. Brown

K. Brown wrote me a letter in regards to this project and I found it so fitting for the ending of the book that I asked him to join us. The following is most of what he wrote.

*   *   *   *   *

Mat,

Those that we served with know what we went through together. We all know what each other went through. I'm talking to all of our brothers and sisters in all the different service branches and in all service duties and positions. I heard a quote once and I admittedly have no clue who said it. I think it was a "dubbya, dubbya deuce" (WWII) general, not sure. They said something along the lines of, "One of two things happen to men when they come back from war. They become better than when they left or they become worse." I don't agree with the word, "worse." They are not worse men. They are suffering men. We have a point of view on this, so let's take a walk for a moment:

I've got it, I know I've got it. I'm not getting help for it because *I like it, I choose to like it*. I like the way it makes me feel. I like thinking about those brave soldiers, each so young and compassionately full of life. So willing. So anxious. So clueless. Innocent is not an appropriate word to use when speaking about, to, or of soldiers so I chose "clueless." I tried to get help for it recently. A few months ago, actually. I went to a professional outside of the VA system who specialized in "PTSD." I visited this guy twice, each time speaking to him for about two hours and getting into some very specific things that happened. We dove headfirst into the detailed reoccurring dreams I have. I talked to him about the feelings I get when I smell certain things or hear certain noises or go out to public places. Even driving on the highway and under overpasses still make me nervous. I told him about how I sometimes get fucking wasted by myself and cry when I'm sitting on my couch, in my house, in Illinois, in the United States of America. That's something I haven't told anyone. I was very honest with this professional man which, I think, enabled me to finally be honest with myself. At the end of the last session I realized I didn't want "help." Why is there a focus on trying to get back to the way we were before the war? Before we deployed? Why are we trying to be "normal" again? This. Is. Fucking. Normal.

For me, this is not about being traumatized by a significant event or a terrible occurrence of gruesome violence or fucked up shit you saw. *It's a God-damn burden.* A very specific type of pride combined with a very unique sense of guilt. It's the carrying of that burden... that relentless, constant, and utmost *beautiful* burden that is what haunts us. And it's what needs to inspire us. The memories of my time in the Army, specifically the men I served with, inspire me. They still motivate me. They always will. They make me *feel.* The feelings that I get remind me that I'm alive and that I have to keep carrying this burden. I must keep carrying this burden... this relentless, constant and most beautifully fucked up burden, because I love it.

If you have "PTSD," embrace it. Don't be ashamed of the things that you've been through. Don't be ashamed of the things that you've seen or loved ones you've lost. Invite these things into your heart, soul and mind in order to help define you. Let them define an inspired, motivated, passionate and alive, YOU. Let them make you stronger. Our suffering should not be considered a disruption, a disability, or even something that would require rehabilitation or God-damn "help." This is our reality now. *A version of our own reality that we can control, construct and build.* We are misunderstanding our own "suffering!" We will never be what we were before war, so stop trying to get back there, for fucks sake. Embrace who you were.

216

Embrace what you've been through. Embrace that you loved the ones that made the ultimate sacrifice. Embrace who you are. Let that burden that is so very beautiful, so very inspiring and so incredibly unique, define you. We will carry this with pride, forever.

I need a drink, a shot even...

Please, raise a glass with me. To all the ones that gave us this gift, this beautiful burden, that we can now use to define ourselves, *Sláinte.*

~K. Brown ~

Charlie Mike

The outreach doesn't stop here and our duty to each other is never done. There will always be war, thus there will always be trauma. We use the term, "Charlie Mike," a lot in the military. It correlates to the letters "C" and "M" in the alphabet. We use a phonetic alphabet to disguise certain messages. Charlie Mike to me, means Continue Mission. If my platoon was attacked and we didn't need to stop what we were originally tasked to do, we would call up on the radio to our troop headquarters that, "We're good to Charlie Mike," and they would understand that we were going to push forward.

The different chalks in this book gave you insight on the subject of PTS(D) through the eyes of people that have seen heavy combat. Some were very close friends and others have no idea who any of the other authors are. All of the opinions are different and all of their experiences can be interpreted or handled differently from everyone else in the book. Then there were unique stories in between each chalk. The insight from these stories are from people that you don't always think about when it comes to war stories. A humble, but open SEAL team member who was able to compare his own experiences to his brother's, who had never been to war. A brother who wrote nothing of his own time in the military, but instead wrote about his brother's, who lost his life. A wife, who will inspire the world to push forward in the face of an unimaginable situation. We've proven that everyone handles every situation differently and treating anyone that is struggling should be done on an individual basis. They should not be simply told that they have PTS(D), get handed meds and then shown the door.

It is our greatest hope that these stories will show people that **you are not alone**. Our focus was on the military, but no matter your trauma, reach out to people that have been through similar circumstances as you. It's human nature not to understand that which you have not experienced, so don't be mad at people who show you no empathy. Look for help in the right places. Also, listen to people looking for your help. You never know what someone has been through until you ask. All 22 authors in this book choose to Charlie Mike. Will you?

A Special Thank You to Our Editors

Below are the super-awesome volunteer editors that put a lot of time and effort into helping this book become what it is. On behalf of all 22 authors, we thank you all!

Chris Howard
Emily Saulsgiver
Jason "Corky" Compton
Jessica Timmerman
Jessica "Vila" LaFever
Joshua Wood
Katie Duckett
K. Brown

Matthew Corbitt
Michleen Lyons Luster
Noah Foreman
Rafael E. Espinal
Stuart Smith
Tara D. Van Horn
Tim Hopkins
Todd P. Landry

A special shout out to my wonderful, beautiful and hilarious wife, ***Alex Vance***. She helped edit this project, created our website and pushed me to the finish line... all while pregnant! To my unborn daughter, Callen, we can't wait to meet you and teach you about fighting the good fights!

You can find us at https://firewithin.online

or

on Facebook as TheFireWithin22.